Dictionary of Today's Landscape Designers

Edited by
Pierluigi Nicolin
Francesco Repishti

Texts
Francesco Repishti

Graphic design
Andrea Lancellotti

Editing
Doriana Comerlati

Layout
Gaetano Cassini

Translation from Italian
Susan Wise

Cover
Marcello Francone

First published in Italy in 2003 by
Skira Editore S.p.A.
Palazzo Casati Stampa
via Torino 61
20123 Milano
Italy
www.skira.net

© 2003 by Skira editore

Printed and bound in Italy.
First edition
ISBN 88-8491-420-5

Distributed in North America
and Latin America by Rizzoli
International Publications, Inc.
through St. Martin's Press, 175 Fifth
Avenue, New York, NY 10010.
Distributed elsewhere in the world
by Thames and Hudson Ltd.,
181a High Holborn, London WC1V
7QX, United Kingdom.

Pierluigi Nicolin
Francesco Repishti

Dictionary of Today's Landscape Designers

Pierluigi Nicolin

New Landscapes: Themes and Configurations

Modern architecture has undeniably endeavoured to establish, among other things, a new, authentic connection with the natural environment. The twentieth-century masters drew up countless projects associating architecture and landscape—we need only think of Frank Lloyd Wright's famous illustrations of organicism and Le Corbusier's poetic rationalism.

The theory of modern architecture, with its appeal to nature as an essential biological factor as well as an ideal of harmony, undoubtedly furthered the development of landscaping. But, as we are well aware, today the transformations of the territory have created an impressive amount of empty, undefinable areas—*terrains vagues*—that the landscape architect has not always succeeded in integrating. When instead he did, as, for instance, in the encounter between Roberto Burle Marx and Le Corbusier, Oscar Niemeyer and Candido Portinari, it led to some masterpieces. Then in the case of Luis Barragán's œuvre, the skills of the architect and the landscape designer merged in a single, exceptional personality. As regards Isamu Noguchi, an atypical artist, his personal conception of landscape evolved when he took part in the experience of post-World War II architecture in America. Behind the revolution the three American architects brought about, we should not overlook their ties with the avant-gardes and their claim to be independent of the methods and tastes of European tradition.

A tempting solution is to arrange the material, now highly complex, of landscape planning (parks, gardens, landscape) in connection with these three acknowledged masters of modern landscaping. The late twentieth century has been much written about and various historiographic approaches are being discussed. Yet it would seem that in the field of landscaping there is a certain agreement to acknowledge the preeminence of certain experiences and, more precisely, to identify Roberto Burle Marx (1909–1994), Luis Barragán (1902–1988), and Isamu Noguchi (1904–1988) as the leading figures of a revolution that led to three approaches, still of consequence today, affecting the entire historical and geographic experience in the development of the "art of gardens".

If we yield to this temptation, looking at the work of the landscape architects featured in this dictionary, rigorously selected to offer an up-to-date survey, we shall be able to discern either the influence of the colourful, wavy touches of Roberto Burle Marx (with his characteristic way of blending avant-garde pictorial research with the form of the landscape), or the walled gardens of Luis Barragán (which combine the idiom of modern and vernacular architecture with the primary elements of nature), or again the contemplative spaces of Isamu Noguchi, with his ability to invent places by his brilliant use of water and carved stones.

We are indeed confronted with a variety of projects expressing an almost boundless range of designs, as we realize as soon as we leaf through the dictionary, yet the frequency of certain issues reduces our sense of having to cope with unwieldy, eclectic information. Several recurrent themes help us see beyond the many differences ascribable to single artistic conceptions and the variety of histories, climates, traditions, circumstances. Rather than simply pointing out differences, our interpretation, in addition to the reference to the mastery of the great twentieth-century landscape architects we just mentioned, bears upon the urgency with which the environmental issue is experienced today, a novel event we shall deal with briefly, in this short introduction.

Our uneasiness over the implications of scientific research in the field of genetic engineering, our concern about the environmental future of the Earth and, in short, everything that has contributed to create a new environmental awareness, such as the idea of sustainable development, our anxiety over the disappearance of animal and plant species, atmospheric pollution, all these have altered our aesthetic view of nature as well. Notions like order and disorder have a different meaning for us compared to a relatively recent past, owing to the importance of the notion of entropy that, as we know, augments with the increase of "orderly" structures. Certainly our appreciation of the wonders of nature is rapidly changing, and we are discovering a landscaping "pluralism" that is producing winning new scenarios for our aesthetic perception: to the "conquest" of mountain and ocean during the eighteenth and nineteenth centuries, we have added the conquest of deserts, tropical forests, underwater areas and, at least in our imagination, cosmological space. Global aesthetization—come about in the day of the image of the world and of the world as image—and the perception of different contexts as authentic eco-systems, induce the landscape architect to challenge the transformative intent of the "design" with an aesthetics of the "as found".

Gilles Clément's recommendation, to support to the utmost possible and oppose the least possible the concrete reality of a given found environmental context, is making headway in a discipline that has a colonizing tradition. In the new landscape designers' research we observe a gradual substitution of references: the usual reference to painting and poetry is completed by direct observation of the various environments of our Earth, examined with a nostalgic, attentive eye. These new interpretative approaches have introduced other scenarios of the Earth in landscape architecture: figures like marshes, evolutive barren lands, tropical forests, deserts, environments characterized by new associations and plant hybridizations. With the decline of the rule of the classical representation of nature, traditionally expressed by the Italian garden or the English park, we observe the rise of several options, both identitary and diasporic. In our field something rather akin to the changed paradigms in anthropology is under way: here, too, we are faced with the effects of decolonization and a series of patterns in which new patriotisms, the desire to produce something "local", merge with global trends and a kind of transnational movement. "If we ask the local population who planted those flowers, they don't know. Have they always been there? But what do nasturtiums, that come from Mexico, have to do with New Zealand? And African arum lilies, rattan from India, that bloom in places far from Africa or from India…? Asiatic hydrangeas and Magellan's fuchsias on the plateaus of La Réunion. Australian and Tanzanian eucalyptus in Africa, in Madagascar, on the Andes, covering barren mountains and inhospitable lands all over the world. Men travelled, and plants went along. This huge mixture, that assembles flowers from continents that have been separated for ages, gives rise to new landscapes."

Another approach to the pluralism of this dictionary might be a pragmatic one, if we envisage the concrete aims of the interventions by examining their effects on the users' fruition. We are clearly dealing with endless possibilities, ranging from the total absence of users in Land Art to participatory operations to stimulate neighbourhood life. One assumption might be to view the tendency to "thematize" as the prevailing form in new landscaping in order to communicate specific values and suggest fruition processes. The garden appears to be a wonderfully suited medium for representing—directly, symbolically or allegorically—the sensibility and the aspirations of a time like ours. A number of characteristic, recurrent themes refer to nature—the arid or Mediterranean garden, etc., or ecological, transgenic, biocompatible; or else to art—figurative, abstract, textural, informal, chaotic, etc.; or social—for children, the disabled, for meditation, for a pause, etc.

We are clearly witnessing the spread of landscaping activities in the most varied countries and situations: this pursuit, hitherto reserved to fervent specialists and deemed marginal—despite modern architects' systematic appeals imposed by a new awareness of the environment—has acquired an unexpected relevance. Yet when, as we can now observe, the means of landscaping, in the wake of the modernist tradition, are widely adopted only as an additive, we end up by taking for granted a merely aesthetizing outcome. The landscape artist, asked to solve the particular problems afflicting the production of local identities in a deterritorialized world, has various techniques at his disposal for producing these local identities: the laying out of paths and passages, the creation and dismantling of fields and vegetable gardens, naming ceremonies, symbolic mapping of areas of transhumance and hunting grounds, all come about in a setting deprived of social actors and housing construction. Called upon to produce or reproduce a local identity, perhaps near the metropolis or alongside a motorway junction, the landscape architect lacks a neighbourhood, meaning an actually existing social form in which the locality, as dimension or value, can be produced in varying degrees. In this case we see that the aesthetizing solution is often the only one, since the clash between the rationale of ecology and of a form of anthropology has not been resolved. A way to produce a neighbourhood would be to encourage a truer fruition of gardens by stimulating, along with play activities, the exercise of upkeeping and cultivating. Taking care of the garden or the vegetable garden can be a way to discover the secrets of nature as well as to confirm the social body, as an alternative to a purely contemplative approach or the extreme option whereby man in nature is an intruder.

There are also times when the conflict can be resolved by integrating the design of the human settlement with the concept of landscape. Rather than asking the landscape architect to complete, remedy or recompose with an aesthetizing action the troublesome situations generated by building practices, the increasingly invasive presence of infrastructures, the functional and formal vagueness of the new public spaces, the trash produced by consumer society, industrial production waste and so on, here the creation of landscape is the starting point and the very purpose of the intervention. Referring to the grand tradition of Frederick Law Olmsted—the famous author of Central Park in New York—Peter Walker requests that landscaping be sufficiently appreciated as to induce the construction of good buildings and good cultivations, and, maybe an even more determining aspect, to upkeep them.

The garden-city and the campus as an organized settlement model arisen from the constitution of the park are well-known antecedents of a principle whereby the landscaper's work prepares the ground for developing the settlement, in an attempt to overcome the cleavage between neighbourhood as social formation and the production of the locality. In this case, we can observe the application of planning notions in circumscribed areas, as in the case of university campuses, scientific-productive parks, new garden-cities ruled by special aesthetic and behavioural codes. Unfortunately even these formations of neighbourhoods seem paradoxical since they create contexts yet at the same time require them. In other words, they inevitably imply the relational awareness of other contexts, but at the same time act as autonomous neighbourhoods, in their interpretation, valorization and material practice.

So producing localities is still problematic in a world that tends to be deterritorialized, diasporic and transnational.

Francesco Repishti

Shifting landscapes

When discussing the different nuances between the words "landscape", "park" and "garden", theoreticians often turn to familiar references, such as, for instance: Cicero's concept of "second nature", the difference between "natural nature" and "artificial nature", the testimonial and evocative significance of the site, the connection with primitive Wilderness, including erudite quotations from Jacopo Bonfadio's *Lettere volgari*, the frescoes by Ambrogio Lorenzetti, the work of Lancelot Capability Brown, Humphry Repton's *Landscape Gardening*, Frederick Law Olmsted's works… These illustrations are very frequently used either to determine the exact limits (not only spatial) and the origin of the notions behind these words, or to attempt to redefine the discipline so as to be able to cope with the "open spaces" of the present-day urban context.

In recent years, the concept of landscape has undergone more changes than ever before. This evolution appears to be gathering such momentum that it often foils the attempt to connect the discipline with history or even with the recent past. Today, *landscape* means a great deal more than the visible features of a territory, and its definition has been extended precisely in order to absorb the conflictual interaction between human activity and the environment. Every physical, human, cultural, social, perceptive and economic element of a landscape has now become a part of the same notion. Currently, the landscape architect is present in environmental planning and large-scale recovery projects for abandoned and residual areas, the design of public spaces and parks, as well as of private gardens, and Land Art and photography. This process has been fostered by an increase in design opportunities and theoretic considerations that, applied to the themes of "sustainability" and environmental and landscape recovery, have brought about a major change in the profession, yielding, in various parts of the world, the earliest hints of a new sensibility. For the first time, the landscaping approach even seems to outweigh the contradictions of the discipline, and is pointed to as a special key for understanding the facts of urbanization and helping to define the city project.

This progress could not fail to involve the agents of these changes as well. Turning their backs on an utterly marginal profession, they developed their research concurrently with the evolution taking place in the arts, urban planning and the concept of public space. Their profession is still blurred, wavering between that of architect, gardener and artist, and still highly diversified, fashioned by a cross-fertilization between nature and architecture, and becoming in many schools an authentic discipline of its own, where very different qualities and sensibilities are encouraged.

For once, this haphazardness and the haziness of the limits of the profession have not been an obstacle, but instead a precise axiom for compiling a *Dictionary of Today's Landscape Designers*. Actually, leafing through these pages, landscaping may seem to be a Babel of languages, "a field explosion", where the themes of landscape and garden are enacted at the same time by Land Art, Earth Art and Minimalism artists along with architects and agronomists, devotees of the historicist rehabilitation of topiaries, as well as by Gilles Clément's theoretic interpretations, which blend landscape and ecology into one, and associate garden and landscape with the biological identity of the environment.

Two references perhaps, more than any others, can help us understand how the "art of gardens" can lead to Martha Schwartz' wonderful landscapes: I do not feel we can fail to examine the results of the Land Art movement (Robert Smithson, Nancy Holt, Mary Miss, Walter De Maria, Tanya Preminger, Michael Heizer, Christo), which for many landscape architects has been a starting point for learning to model the ground, and which above all was a new step contributing to erode the separations between the arts and to further interdisciplinary collaboration. And then it would be unthinkable to pass over the works of Luis Barragán, Roberto Burle Marx and the *scenarios* built by Isamu Noguchi.

Possible grounds for exploring the production of the over eighty landscape designers appearing in this book might be the differences and likenesses in their training, owing to certain schools or ways of thinking closely bound to their native cultural traditions, either American, Oriental or European. In America the profession evolved along with the artistic trends, which became a constant source of inspiration and of models. Expressed in the landscape, they turned into pattern, texture, objects, compositions of complex systems. Minimalism, Land Art, Abstraction, Pop Art and Organicism merged into a specific art in which colours, materials, forms are laid out, revealing and transfiguring the nature and the shape of places. Peter Walker's Minimalist gardens showed the way for Martha Schwartz' Pop experiments, for George Hargreaves' deconstructionism on a territorial scale and Kathryn Gustafson's quotations, while Richard Haag deals with the theme of environmental reclamation and Walter Hood with the rehabilitation of the cityscape in view of a social revival. Japanese gardens, still inspired by the harmony of the Zen tradition, reveal great mastery in the art of inlay, of building, inventing and placing objects combined with the particular form and the strong sense of the site, conceived as a meaningful space rather than a mere setting.

But if the first two geographic contexts, to make a rather facile generalization, seem after all to be homogeneous, the European context reflects a designing and executive ebullience in which it seems almost impossible to classify the contemporary trends. Next to the French school, whose theoretic base can be found in the research of Augustin Berque, Pierre Donadieu and Alain Roger, along with the anything but monolithic Ecole Supérieure du Paysage in Versailles, we have the Dutch Rem Koolhaas' vision of "diffused space", Adriaan Geuze's originality and schematic German geometrism, or the revisited and occasionally "over-correct" Mediterranean tradition, as well as the historicism of the Belgian school and that of Jacques Wirtz.

In Italy, on the other hand, bound to the idea of the garden as nature in nature, the notion of landscape and garden is still frozen. So the practically total absence of contemporary Italian landscape designers does not come as a surprise, since they are hidden in the bucolic retreats of private patrons rather than being involved in the everyday building of cities. Reviewing the works carried out in the past ten years is like outlining a geography composed of "dispersed author's places". The Italian context reflects a substantial operational scepticism, or else naturalistic and conservatory extremes.

The approach to the theme suggested in this dictionary is not a study of the various, easily identified schools. It is intrinsically bound to the contemporary status of the profession, and intentionally does not treat the notion of the garden as "art in the landscape", nor the historical surveys found in most of the books on the subject. Nor is it bound to an exclusively urban view of the landscape. Instead it sets store by the idea that landscape is above all a cultural invention, a transformation of a place that can be brought about by a concrete, direct intervention or else by an indirect aesthetic recognition referring to models of vision and artistic models or to perceptive patterns (actually to the eye, which, in observing a place—or its image—composes and ascribes the significance of a landscape). Environment in itself does not constitute a landscape (so it should not have an implicit beauty), and the garden is not the only place appointed to make explicit this beauty. Sometimes the very absence of "greenery" is not a lack of landscape: instead, as Bernard Lassus already pointed out, "it is not at all inconceivable that a polluted place can form a beautiful landscape and that, vice versa, an unpolluted place may not necessarily be beautiful".

A present-day debate that seems to lead less to an accurate definition than to an idea of "shifting landscapes"—extending the limits of Gilles Clément's fine intuition—overcoming that which, in the early nineties, seemed to many to have become uncertain and wavering between sculpture and the naturalistic vision.

This obviously lies behind our decision not to discuss the essence of the theme, but to suggest the different ways of creating a landscape and to acknowledge that the constant enrichment of our landscape vision creates a range of new landscapes, not just material (underground, marine, planetary), but virtual as well (Kengo Kuma), olfactory (Nathalie Poiret), sonorous (Murray Schafer), photographic (Alex MacLean, Eliot Porter) and luminous (Motoko Ishii). Without overlooking possible thematic approaches, besides the naturalistic ones, that involve patrons and future users: along with gardens inspired by the tradition of the *hortus botanicus* (Lothar Baumgarten), we have therapeutic gardens (Douglas Reed), gardens for religious communities (Delaney & Cochran), "social" landscapes (Walter Hood), spaces to pause in and to go through, totem-gardens for multinational companies…

So the aim of this book is to illustrate the different ways of understanding landscape, creating a dictionary that can not only convey the scope of the designing processes and the people behind them, but also provide a first key for interpreting the various approaches to this research, which has given rise to an entirely new dimension in designing the cityscape, turning the open space of the city into a space for art and sculpture, for garden and architecture, and into a new field for cultural activity.

The dictionary is arranged in strictly alphabetical order. The two introductory essays explaining the approach and the objectives of the book are followed by the documentation on the architects, engineers, landscapers, artists, photographers, from various schools and cultural backgrounds, whose work contributes to define the present-day survey of research on this theme. Each author is presented with a biographical note, the list of his/her works and related bibliography, and several images illustrating the most significant designs.

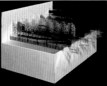

F

G

H

IJ

RS

TU

VWZ

A

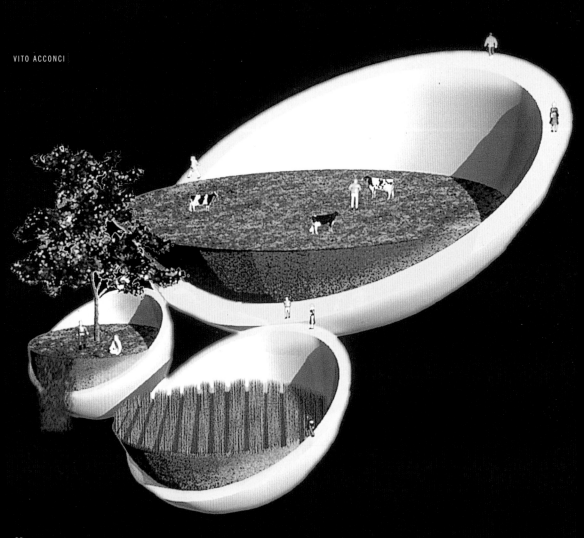

Vito Acconci

Usa

1940

*A City That Rides
the Garbage Dump,*
Ravel Tip, Breda, 1999.

*Flying Floors
to Ticketing Pavilion,*
Philadelphia Airport,
1998.

Artist and urban landscape architect. He began in art as a novelist and a poet, writing stories based on puns, using the page as a limited space to overcome. In the late sixties and early seventies, he chose performance, film and video as instruments for self-analysis and for creating interpersonal relationships. During the seventies and the eighties, his audio and video installations turned exhibition spaces into meeting places, and with his "participative sculpture" he created representational spaces. Toward the mid-eighties, he turned to making architecture maquettes and to landscape architecture; he opened an architecture studio, Acconci Studio, that designs public areas—streets and plazas, gardens and parks, building entrance halls and transportation centres—and exhibitions, furnishings and vehicles, either theoretic, or feasible for building, always involving the human presence.

Park up a Building, 1996.

Projects Plaza, Midwest Convention Center, Milwaukee; Mobile Garden, Building Department Administration, Munich; Linear Mobile City, 1991 (Biennial of Architecture, Venice, 2000); Personal Island, Zoetemeer, Netherlands, 1992; Loloma Transportation Center, Scottsdale, Arizona, 1995–97; Park up a Building, Santiago de Compostela, Spain, 1996; Screens for a Walkway, Shibuya Station, Tokyo, 1996–2000; Flying Floors, Philadelphia Airport, Philadelphia, 1998; Seats for the 161st Street Subway Station, Bronx, New York, 2000. **Selected bibliography** *Vito Acconci: Making Public,* The Hague, 1993; *Vito Acconci: The City Inside Us,* Vienna, 1993; *Vito Acconci,* edited by K. Linker, New York, 1994; *Art News, Daidalos, Domus, Lotus international, Landscape Architecture, Land Forum.*

"Space as an image you become part of,
space as an occasion for behaviour"

EMILIO AMBASZ

Emilio Ambasz

Argentina
1943

In transposing his experience as designer and interpreter of the contemporary domestic scene onto the larger scale of architectural design (he curated the exhibition "Italy: The New Domestic Landscape" at the MoMA in New York, 1971), Emilio Ambasz explores the complex relationships between nature and artifice, memory and innovation. His buildings hint at a connection with geology and archaeology: they are etched, camouflaged in the territory, or loom over it like huge cristals. In their explicit techno-ecological connotation they comprise vast areas permeated with nature, seeking to create a sense of wonderment and visual disorientation. In the Schlumberger Research Laboratories, the laboratories and researchers' offices, arrayed around an artificial lake, crop up like geological strata, suggesting a landscape where "primitive" and "civilized" merge, steeped in allegorical references. In the design to organize the area of La Venta, in Mexico City, the office buildings, with rooftop nurseries for the reafforestation of the surrounding wooded area, remind us of pre-Columbian settlements, recalling the cosmological incisions throughout the American territory.

EMILIO AMBASZ

02

Résidence au Lac, Lugano.

Jardins de la France, Chaumont-sur-Loire, France.

La Venta, Mexico City.

Works and projects Schlumberger Research Laboratories, Austin, Texas; Mycal Cultural Center, Shin-Anda, Japan; Prefectural International Hall, Fukuoka, Japan; Lucille Halsell Conservatory, San Antonio, Texas; Terrace, Résidence au Lac, Lugano, Switzerland; Residence and Private Art Gallery, Montana; Financial Guaranty Insurance Company, New York; Worldbridge Trade and Investment Center, Baltimore, Maryland; Houston Center Plaza, Houston, Texas; Jardins, Festival de Chaumont-sur-Loire, France. **Exhibitions** "Dieci anni di architettura, graphic e industrial design", Milan, 1983, Madrid-Zurich, 1984; "Architecture", Museum of Modern Art, New York, 1989 (Tokyo, 1993); "Architecture, Exhibition, Industrial and Graphic Design", San Diego, Montreal, Chicago, St. Louis, 1989; "Architettura e design", Milan Triennial, 1995. **Selected bibliography** E. Ambasz, *Emilio Ambasz: The Poetics of the Pragmatic*, New York, 1988; E. Ambasz, *Architettura e design*, Milan 1994. His works have been published in the reviews *Architectural Record*, *Architecture plus Urbanism*, *Domus*, *On*, *Space and Design*.

SVEN-INGVAR ANDERSSON

Sven-Ingvar Andersson

Sweden
1927

Gustav Adolf Plaza,
Malmö, 1997.

Scanpark,
Copenhagen, 1996.

An authority in Scandinavia since the early seventies, his work reflects his endeavour to integrate the gardener's competencies with the understanding of ecological issues and trends in contemporary art. His professional training began concretely by gardening, followed by studies aiming at developing both creative and technical abilities. Sven-Ingvar Andersson's works testify that his approach to the theme is strongly motivated by the values of social and ethical commitment, in which landscape architecture is a pursuit associating architecture, art, sociology and ecology. The precision and bareness of the space blend harmoniously with the preciousness of the elements and plant essences. He taught landscape architecture at the Architecture School of the Fine Arts Academy of Copenhagen from 1963 to 1994.

03

Works Archives of Decorative Arts, Lund, Sweden, 1958; The Gullestrup Plan, Denmark, 1968; Karlsplatz-Reeselpark, Vienna, 1971–78, 1987; Damsgård Hage, Bergen, Norway, 1983; Österåker Cemetery, Sweden, 1983; Tête, La Défense, Paris, 1984; Ronneby Spa, Sweden, 1986; Gardens and Craftmanship, Stockholm, 1988; Sankt Hans Museumsplein, Copenhagen, 1992; Uranienborg, Island of Hven, Denmark, 1992–93; Christiansbro Urban Space, Denmark, 1995; Aolo Golf Club, Italy, 1995; Scanpark, Copenhagen, 1996; The Railway Environment, Lund, Sweden, 1997; Gustav Adolf Plaza, Malmö, Sweden, 1997; University of Frankfurt am Main, 1997; The Citadel, Copenhagen, 1997; Museumplein, Amsterdam, 1999. **Selected bibliography** U. Weilacher, *Between Landscape Architecture and Land Art*, Berlin, 1996; G. Cooper, G. Taylor, *Gardens for the Future*, New York, 2000. His works have been published in the reviews *Architettura del paesaggio*, *Landskab*, *Topos*, *Utblick Landskap*.

Tadao Ando

Japan
1941

The role of Tadao Ando's architecture is to create new landscapes: the building becomes the setting where all the natural elements are represented and reduced—the light of day and of the seasons, the wind, water, trees...—his inside space is thought of as a place that both separates and connects man with nature and with himself. So, Ando's works are meant to constantly appeal to the sensitivity and the emotions of those who use them. This quest for spirituality and meditation is the matrix of all his major works, either in the construction of closed, intimate spaces, private gardens, or the deliberate naturalness of the larger architectures. Tadao Ando's work always reveals surprising, novel approaches to reality: whether it be the materials used, the plain geometric forms or the use of light as an important factor to control and measure the invented spaces. Since the late eighties he has been Visiting Professor in various American universities. One-man shows of

his work have been mounted at the MoMA of New York (1991), the Centre Pompidou of Paris and the RIBA of London (1993), in Barcelona and Vicenza (1994–95), Seoul and London (1998) and Berlin (1999).

TADAO ANDO

04

Chikatsu-Asuka Historical Museum, Osaka, 1994.

Nariva Museum, Okayama, 1994 (Shigeo Ogawa Photo).

Works Row House, Sumiyoshi, Osaka, Japan, 1976; Rokko Housing I, Kobe, Japan, 1983; Time's, Kyoto, Japan, 1984; Church of the Light, Osaka, Japan, 1989; Museum of Literature, Himeji, Japan, 1991; Water Temple, Awajishima, Japan, 1991; Japan Pavilion Expo '92, Seville, Spain, 1992; Naoshima Contemporary Art Museum & Annex, Kagawa, Japan, 1992–95; Rokko Housing II, Kobe, Japan, 1993; Chikatsu-Asuka Historical Museum, Osaka, Japan, 1994; Suntory Museum, Osaka, Japan, 1994; Mikata-Gun, Hyogo, Japan, 1994; Meditation Space, Unesco, Paris, 1995; Toto Seminar House, Awaji Island, Hyogo, Japan, 1998; Daylight Museum, Gamo-Gun, Japan, 1998; Rokko Housing III, Kobe, Japan, 1999; Awaji-Ymebutai, Tsuna-Gun, Japan, 2000. **Monographs** K. Frampton, *Tadao Ando: Buildings, Projects, Writings*, New York, 1984; F. Dal Co, *Tadao Ando. Le opere, gli scritti*, Milan, 1994; M. Furuyama, *Tadao Ando*, Basel-Boston, 1995 (Zurich, 1993; Barcelona, 1994; Bologna, 1997); P. Jodidio, *Tadao Ando*, Cologne, 1997. His works have been published in all the leading reviews including *Casabella*, *Croquis*, *GA Architects*, *Lotus international*.

Museum of Wood,
Mikata-Gun, Hyogo, 1994
(Mitsuo Matsuoka Photo).

Children's Museum,
Hyogo, 1989
(Mitsuo Matsuoka Photo).

Church on the Water,
Yufutsu-Gun, Hokkaido, 1988
(Mitsuo Matsuoka Photo).

"What I have sought to achieve is a spatiality that stimulates the human spirit, awakens the sensitivity and communicates with the deeper soul"

APRILE, COLLOVÀ, LA ROCCA

Marcella Aprile
Roberto Collovà
Teresa La Rocca

Italy

The project arose from a commission they received in 1982 from the Town Administration of Gibellina, a newly founded town that was built at some distance from the old centre, after the 1968 earthquake. The Di Stefano Houses—a fortified farm, common in the Sicilian countryside—to make up for the lack of roots of the new town, was appointed "historic centre", lying outside the walls of a destroyed town twenty kilometres away. Using the fragmentary remains, still closely bound to the surroundings and more remote buildings, an articulated ensemble—consisting of courtyards, a walkway, an external esplanade, a network of paths, roads and inner ways, open and covered galleries, and connected with the access road and other spaces and more distant roads—fashioned an unusual relationship between the old structure of the hamlet and the surrounding landscape; a network joining close elements and the more remote landscape that is drawn into the new ensemble. The parking area is the largest surface of this new "built ground": it was made by digging the ground uphill and moving it downhill, forming an artificial hill that masks it from close up.

Di Stefano Houses,
Gibellina, 1982–98.

Projects Rehabilitation project of the town and of the Mother Church, Salemi, 1982 (Collovà); Outdoors Theatre, Salemi, 1982 (with F. Venezia); Rehabilitation plan of the Cascio neighbourhood, Salemi (1990). **Selected bibliography** *Casabella*, *Domus*, *Lotus international*.

B

KARL BAUER

Karl Bauer

Germany
1940

Landscape architect. Trained at the Technical University of Karlsruhe and a pupil of Gunnar Martinsson, Karl Bauer seeks to express in his works the present-day precariousness of greenery areas in big cities. For Bauer, the architect's mission is to create bold open spaces that counteract, or complete, extend or improve the features of the built areas. At Melsungen, Albstadt and Karlsruhe trees become the essential matrix of the design: they are isolated in large artificial flowerbeds, "built" like simple natural rooms and like landscapes carved out of the dense built fabric or between the areas reserved for parking. Actually trees lend themselves in many ways to the organization of architectural space: they require but a small surface, yet on the other hand they take up a large volume in the air and, with their appearance that changes with the seasons, they bring variety to the area throughout the year. However, the geometric planted islands Bauer designs do not dialogue with the buildings, since they represent nature opposed to architecture.

Braun AG Landscape Park, Mesulgen, 1992.

Südwestliche Bau-Berufs-Genossenschaft Grounds, Karlsruhe, 1992.

Works Park der Industrieanlage Braun, Melsungen, Germany, 1987–92; Fachhochschule Grounds, Albstadt-Ebingen, Germany, 1989–92; Südwestliche Bau-Berufs-Genossenschaft, Karlsruhe, Germany, 1990–92; Stadtteilpark Heilbronn-Böckingen, Heilbronn, Germany, 1995; Freianlagen für Verwaltungsgebäude, Karlsruhe, Germany; Begrünung des Dachens eines Verwaltungsgebäudes, Ettlingen, Germany; Rahmenplanung für den Universitätsbereich Stuttgart-Vaihingen, Germany; Wettbewerb Bundesgartenschau, Karlsruhe, Germany. **Selected bibliography** His works have been published in the reviews *Architektur + Wettbewerbe*, *Garten und Landschaft*, *Landscape Design*, *Topos*.

LOTHAR BAUMGARTEN

Lothar Baumgarten

Germany
1944

Lothar Baumgarten inherited his anthropologist father's curiosity for all those cultures "different" from the European one, precisely directing his artistic research—travels, films, photographs, art works, installations and gardens—toward bringing the different civilizations closer. Recently for the Fondation Cartier he designed their headquarters' garden, inspired, as its name "Theatrum Botanicum" clearly states, by the Medieval codexes where the monks classified plant species, both officinal for curing diseases, and aromatic for cooking. So, although the scattering of the plant and tree essences appears to be random, the Paris garden is an artfully cultivated garden, a *hortus conclusus* (concretely closed by walls, glass partitions and metal fences), recalling the roots of the renaissance of European culture. But the Theatrum Botanicum is not just a garden of remembrance or a modern herbarium. Its contemporaneity is particularly illustrated by its "social" composition, hosting a number of native and foreign plant species—nearly a hundred and fifty—and by the different layout of the areas forming it, inspired by the nature and composition of the soil.

Fondation Cartier,
Paris, 2000.

Exhibitions Documenta V, Kassel, 1972; Documenta VII, Kassel, 1982; "L'époque, la mode, la morale, la passion. Aspects de l'art d'aujourd'hui", 1977–87, Centre Pompidou, Paris; Documenta IX, Kassel, 1992; Documenta X, Kassel, 1997; "Change of scene XIV", Frankfurt am Main, 1998; "Lothar Baumgarten. Das druckgraphische Werk 1978–1998", Zurich, 1998–99; "The Museums as Muse: Artists Reflect", MoMA, New York, 1999. **Selected bibliography** *Accès aux quais: tableaux parisiens*, Paris, 1986; *Makunaima*, New York, 1987; *Carbon*, Los Angeles-Pentti Kouri, 1991; *America*, New York, 1993; *Lothar Baumgarten. Eklipse*, Düsseldorf, 1997.

PETRA BLAISSE

Petra Blaisse

Netherlands

1955

Museumpark,
Rotterdam, 1994.

*Gardens for the
Stedelijk Museum,*
Amsterdam, 1992.

*Glasshouse
& Recreation Area,*
Harmelerwaard, 1994.

In 1991 Petra Blaisse opened her own design studio, Inside Outside, specializing in combining inside and outside spaces. While investigating this traditional relationship, Blaisse developed a new vocabulary, introducing the use of movement and challenging the conventional distinctions between those spaces: her work's main objectives are to connect inside and outside and mingle architecture and lansdcape. The designs for inside, in spite of the soft materials they are made of, are interventions that can alter the perception of the architectural context. The designs for outside spaces reflect a like fascination for unusual materials and astonishing combinations of colours and forms. Her gardens often feature reflective materials, lighting effects and curtaining, along with large stretches of grass and flowering plants laid out in a design with shifting colours. She drew international attention with her theatre curtains, acoustic walls and cast pavings, and her White Orchard—the ninety metres-long mirror wall and the glass river—created for the Rotterdam Museumpark.

Inside Outside, Nieuwegein,
1999.

Works Gardens for the Stedelijk Museum, Amsterdam, 1992 (with Oma); Museumpark, Rotterdam, Netherlands, 1992–94 (with Oma); Roof Garden Kunsthal, Rotterdam, 1993 (with Oma); Glasshouse & Recreation Area, Harmelerwaard, Netherlands, 1994; Landscape design, Chin Suei Service Area, Taiwan, 1996 (with M. Botta, Oma, J. Nouvel, T. Farnell); Landscape design, H-Project, Seoul, Korea, 1996 (with Oma); Artillerie Terrein, Arnhem, Netherlands, 1997; Landscape design, Headquarters Building, Los Angeles, 1997–99 (with Oma); Roofgarden around Parking, Rijswijk, Netherlands, 1998; Inside Outside, Nieuwegein, Netherlands, 1999 (with Archivolt Architekten); Garden for Parking Park, Almere, 1999; Garden Chasse Terrein, Breda, 1999–2000 (with X. de Geyter); Public park design, Niederlandische Botschaft, Berlin, 2000 (with Oma); Seattle Public Library, Seattle, Washington, 2000 (with Oma); UCLA Hammer Museum, Los Angeles, California (with M. Maltzan and B. Mau). **Selected bibliography** *Architectural Record, Metropolis, Oase Tijdschrift voor Architectuur.*

Just : a matter of : shifting and adding rediscovering and layering : givens :
link shrink tear seam steam overlap : overlay widen lighten pleat :
knot knit : button zip snap plant place : grow fasten : drop feel feed clean
hear hold fumble press stroke : weave line cross bridge swallow : open :

to : shift to add readapt and colour: predict deform refold combine place print stitch stick adhere crumble burn dip cook salt spray puff cut : weed seed root grow : cure pot : rot pat see plot : read smell plan name enlarge refine : re-define speak out : inside outside"

EDUARD BRU I BISTUER

Eduard
Bru i Bistuer

Spain
1950

Olympic Area of Vall d'Hebrón, Barcelona, 1994.

Of all the works Eduard Bru designed and built, the Olympic Area of the Vall d'Hebrón is the one that more than any other suggests the idea of the park as a large collective area, not a space for contemplation, but a place "where you are always doing something: running, skating or dancing. You don't look at it, you come and go in it". Actually, the purpose of the intervention is to provide the city with recreational places, laid out so that outdoors activities prevail over large containers. It is a huge agora for metropolitan recreation featuring elements inviting a stroll and areas for sitting, games for children, a belvedere and narrow passageways, sidewalks, roads and paths from where you can look out over the large playgrounds. "An unusual artificial landscape, based on the singular combination of the idea of a park with equipment and the road network of a garden city where pedestrians and automobiles can freely intersect."

Works (a selection) Area of the Alhambra of Granada, Spain; Master plan of the Autonomous University of Barcelona; Centro de Menors Difícils, Palau de Plegamants, Spain, 1984; Olympic Area of the Vall d'Hebrón, Barcelona, 1989-92; Zoo of Cordova, Spain, 1991. **Selected bibliography** E. Bru i Bistuer, V. Fisher, *Barcelona - Neue Architekturtendenzen*, Berlin, 1996; E. Bru, *Ciutat real, ciutat ideal: significat i funciò a l'espai modern*, Barcelona, 1998; E. Bru, *Housing. New Alternatives, New Systems*, Barcelona, 1998; E. Bru, *New Landscapes, New Territories*, Barcelona, 1998; *World of Environmental Design*, edited by F. Asensio Cerver, Barcelona, 1998; *AMC, Archis, Architectural Review, A+U, Casabella, El Croquis, Lotus international, Quaderns d'arquitectura i urbanisme, Rassegna*.

WILLIAM P. BRUDER

William P. Bruder

Usa
1946

An architect and sculptor, he worked with Gunnar Birkerts and Paolo Soleri. His creative and disciplinary choices point to clear affinities with the "Californian school", especially apparent in his interest in the interaction between architecture and environment, in his lack of formal or stylistic pre-conceptions and his striking fondness for texture in his architectures, authentic building performances. On the outside his works are laid out like an artificial complement to the topography of the land, adopting a facing that, going beyond the traditional notions of wall, frame, plugging, facing, façade and roof, actually becomes a form of expression. The materials he uses, even second-hand ones, recall industrial aesthetics: the manifestation of an intimate principle conveying an impression of the precariousness and impermanence of the installation, a sense of its temporary occupation of the land, of its being both extraneous to nature and in harmony with it, without yielding to the least vernacular nostalgia.

He has been Visiting Professor, professor and critic for several institutions, including the Massachusetts Institute of Technology and the universities of Oklahoma and Arizona.

WILLIAM P. BRUDER

10

*Deer Valley
Rock Art Center*,
Phoenix, Arizona.

Works (a selection) Central Library, Phoenix, Arizona; Deer Valley Rock Art Center, Phoenix, Arizona; Scottsdale Art Center Addition, Scottsdale, Arizona. **Selected bibliography** W. Bruder, *The Magic of Materials and Light: the Architecture of William P. Bruder*, Portland, 1988; *Architectural Record*, *Architectural Review*, *A+U*, *Interior Design*, *L'Architecture d'aujourd'hui*, *Lotus international*, *Metropolis*, *Progressive Architecture*, *Ville e Giardini*.

Yves Brunier

France

1962-1991

After graduating in 1986 at Versailles, a few years later he began to collaborate as landscape architect in projects executed by Rem Koolhaas-Oma and by Jean Nouvel. Yves Brunier, in the five years of his short career, was one of the most interesting figures among the French landscapers who were to influence a great number of contemporary works. In his designs, the choices he made are the application to landscape of particular architectural principles, achieved without ever generalizing this discipline but adjusting it to the contexts. At Tours, at Rotterdam and in the operations for the rehabilitation of the banks of the Adour River at Dax, his gardens seem above all to be "mental spaces", occasionally interpreted as ambitious, renewed visions of the present-day world: the appeal to the imagination, even fairy-tale like, and the suggestive power of certain images form and even further a subtle dialogue on the reality of things. Occasionally his approach to "naturalness" seems aggressive, as if the place had to be stripped of its natural character to become an expressionist object.

YVES BRUNIER

11

Banks of the Adour,
Dax, 1991–92.

Projects Ville Nouvelle, Melun-Sénart, France, 1987; Gardens of Hôtel Saint-James, Bordeaux, 1987–89; Park of Hôtel du departément de la Vendée, La Roche-sur-Yon, France, 1988–90; Zac Evangile, Paris, 1988; Waterloo, Belgium, 1989; Museumpark, Rotterdam, Netherlands, 1989–91; Nursery School Yard, Evian-les-Bains, France, 1989; Château Canon la Gaffelière, Saint-Emilion, 1989; Euralille City Park, Lille, France, 1989–91; Place du Général Leclerc, Tours, France, 1989–92; Banks of the Vilaine, Rennes, France, 1990; Villa dall'Ava, Saint-Cloud, France, 1990–91; Three private gardens, Belgium, 1991; Banks of the Adour, Dax, France, 1991–92. **Selected bibliography** *Yves Brunier. Paysagiste*, edited by M. Jacques, Berlin, 1996; *Yves Brunier. Landscape Architect*, Bordeaux, 1996; I. Cortesi, *Il parco pubblico. Paesaggi 1985–2000*, Milan, 2000; *L'Architecture d'aujourd'hui, Topos, 2G.*

DANIEL BUREN

Daniel Buren

France

1938

His early works come under the heading of Conceptual Art; ever since his first exhibition in Paris in 1966, painting was reduced to a sequence of vertical bands, a "zero degree", uniform and neutral, offering countless repetitions and susceptible to being reproduced on a variety of supports. Over the years his approach to art has remained substantially the same, whereas the dialectic relationship with the context wherein he places his works has grown increasingly complex. His interventions in city spaces, like streets, underground stations, gardens and museums enhance, emphasize, and "measure" the space, making use of various types of supports. They appear as an attraction, something that brings out the particular nature of the site. His interventions nearly always produce ephemeral works, featuring a description and offering an unusual landscape, emphasizing its character in a special connotation, either in affinity or in opposition with the place itself: so the pictures that document an installation are inevitably souvenir-snapshots and cannot replace the artist's work.

Emprunter le paysage, Ushimado, 1985.

Structure for two catalpas, Serpentine Gallery, London, 1987.

Emprunter le paysage, Ushimado, 1985.

Permanent works (a selection) Les Deux Plateaux, Palais Royal, Paris; Déplacement - Jaillissement: d'une fontaine les autres, Place des Terreaux, Lyon, France; Sens dessus-dessous, Parc des Célestins, Lyon, France; 25 porticos: la couleur et ses reflets, Odaiba, Tokyo. **Selected bibliography** *Daniel Buren: points de vue*, Paris, 1983; C. Francblin, *Daniel Buren*, Paris, 1987; *Daniel Buren. Photo-Souvenirs 1965–1988*, Turin-Villeurbanne, 1988; *Im Raum: Die Farbe. Arbeiten in situ von Daniel Buren*, Vienna, 1989; *Daniel Buren*, Stuttgart, 1990; *Daniel Buren. El color y su reflejo*, Madrid, 1990; *Daniel Buren. Les Ecrits (1965–1990)*, Bordeaux, 1991; *Daniel Buren. Arguments topiques*, Bordeaux, 1991; D. Buren, M. Parmentier, *Propos délibérés*, Brussels 1991; *Daniel Buren. Erscheinen, scheinen, verschwinden*, Düsseldorf, 1996; *Daniel Buren. Trasparence de la lumière. Travaux in situ*, Mito (Japan), 1996; *Daniel Buren. Images du Japon*, Paris, 1996; *A force de descendre dans la rue, l'art peut-il enfin y monter?*, Paris, 1998; *Daniel Buren. Colour-Transparency. Cabanes éclatées n° 26a and 26b*, Frankfurt am Main, 1999; D. Buren, *L'ineffable, à propos de l'œuvre de Ryman*, Paris, 1999; *Cabanes éclatées 1975–2000*, Paris, 2000.

C

FERNANDO CARUNCHO

Fernando Caruncho

Spain

1957

Ollauri Garden,
Rioja, 1987.

Mas de les Voltes,
Castel de Ampurdán,
1997.

Caruncho Garden,
Madrid, 1989.

Fernando Caruncho's gardens are deceptively simple: they use a relatively small number of plants, are often laid out on a geometric grid and feature a limited colour range. But behind this simplicity there is a refined, unique designing method grounded in the theories of the great historic gardens of the Western and Arabic tradition, and in Caruncho's subtle philosophical dialogue on the concept of "time". A gardener—as he is fond of calling himself—and not a landscape designer, Caruncho believes the garden is a space to transform and uplift the human spirit. His works, mostly private gardens, recall formal gardens by their apparently formal structure, yet they harmonize and mingle native forms, elements and essences, typical of either historic or contemporary gardens, with the various sites.

Works Private garden, Aravaca, 1979–81; Mas Floris Garden, Masos de Pals, 1984–86; Ollauri Garden, La Rioja, 1985–87; Jardín S'Agaro, Costa Brava, 1987; Rosales Garden, La Florida, Madrid, 1987–88; Caruncho Garden, Madrid, 1988–89; Albouy Garden, Barcelona, 1988–89; Fiunchal Garden, Vigo, 1988–89; Sotogrande Garden, Marbella, 1988–89; Pazo Pegullal, Salceda de Caselas, Vigo, 1988–2000; University of Deusto, Bilbao, 1989–90; Camp Sarch, Minorca, 1989–90; Saorin Garden, Madrid, 1989–91; Marañon Garden, Madrid, 1990–91; Carvajal-Marquez Garden, Majorca, 1991–92; Ardila Garden, Madrid, 1991–93; Jardín in la Moraleja, Madrid, 1992–93; El Viso Garden, Madrid, 1993–94; Teknon Clinic, Barcelona, 1993–94; La Gerezieta, Biarritz, 1994–96; Postigo Garden, Madrid, 1994–97; Mas de les Voltes, Castel de Ampurdán, 1995–97; Cabo de Formentor, Majorca, 1996–97; Extension of the Real Jardín Botánico, Madrid; Garden of the Spanish Embassy in Tokyo, 2000–. **Selected bibliography** G. Cooper, G. Taylor, *Paradise Transformed. The Private Garden for the Twenty-First Century*, New York, 1996; *Mirrors of Paradise. The Gardens of Fernando Caruncho*, New York, 2000; G. Cooper, G. Taylor, *Gardens for the Future*, New York, 2000.

13

Mas Floris,
Masos de Pals, 1984–86.

University of Deusto,
Bilbao, 1989–90.

ALEXANDRE CHEMETOFF

**Alexandre
Chemetoff**

France
1950

Acclaimed as an architect for his landscaping activity and now known for his urban projects, Chemetoff sees the context he is working in as the very source of the design rather than a contingency to adapt, acknowledging its traditional forms while building its new use. In 1985 Tschumi invited him to create a thematic garden called the Garden of Energy at La Villette; Chemetoff decided to introduce in this area of the park a hollow space where a botanic species, bamboo, confronts an artificial human product, concrete. So the Jardin des Bambous (Bamboo Garden), an authentic "climatic theatre" and a "manifesto of leaves and concrete", sums up the approach to an art that opposes and combines the skill of the botanist with modern technology. His latest projects engage him in designing residual urban lots located on the outskirts, or as landscape architect in new towns (La Courneuve, Zac at Nancy), or in the rehabilitation of areas for recreation (the seafront promenade at Le Havre).

14

Promenades des Régates,
Le Havre, 1996.

Jardin des Bambous,
Parc de La Villette,
Paris, 1985–87.

Works Garden of the French Embassy, New Delhi, India, 1983–86; Jardin des Bambous, Parc de La Villette, Paris, 1985–87; Jardin d'Eau, Zac Stanislas-Meurthe, Nantes, France, 1989; Beach of Le Havre, France, 1989–; Place de la Bourse, Lyon, France, 1992–95; Parc public et des Ports Géo-André, La Courneuve, France, 1993; Parc des Saules, Orly, France, 1994–98; Promenades des Régates, Le Havre, France, 1996–. **Selected bibliography** S. Lyall, *Designing the New Landscape*, London, 1991; L. Baljon, *Designing Parks*, Amsterdam, 1992; A. Chemetoff, *Le Jardin des Bambous au parc de La Villette*, Paris, 1997; A. Chemetoff, B. Lemoine, *Sur les quais. Un point de vue parisien*, Paris, 1998; M. Hucliez, *Jardins et parcs contemporains*, Paris, 1999; G. Donin, *Parchi/Parks*, Cannitello (Villa San Giovanni, Italy), 1999; I. Cortesi, *Il parco pubblico. Paesaggi 1985–2000*, Milan, 2000; *A+U*, *Architectural Review*, *Arquitectura Viva*, *Casabella*, *L'Architecture d'aujourd'hui*, *Lotus international*, *Topos*.

"The Bamboo Garden is a manifesto of leaves and concrete. My training as a city gardener led me to become fond of concrete, the kind that is neither smoothed, nor architectural, but rough, used in some works of art, and evocative of territory"

SUSAN CHILD

Susan Child

Usa

Grand Isle Residence,
Lake Champlain,
Vermont, 1991.

South Cove, Battery
Park City, New York, 1988
(Cymie Payne Photo).

Esplanade Roof Terrace,
Cambridge,
Massachusetts, 1991.

After winning worldwide acclaim for her work at South Cove (Battery Park) in New York—executed with Mary Miss and Douglas Reed—in her projects she seems to prefer the construction of new natural landscapes that are grafted like works of art onto the complexity of the urban environment. These are operations that truly recreate the open space with the aim of achieving highly representative images, also connoting the new spaces as referential sites, functional in public life. Therefore not a self-centred art, but one that, precisely thanks to its social and recreational role, furthers participatory actions and reactions. Today Susan Child and Associates is one of the most important design studios for landscapes and gardens, with its premises in Boston. Her latest projects concern the master plan for the new Botanical Gardens of New York and for Cornell University at Ithaca.

15

Works South Cove, Battery Park City, New York, 1988 (with M. Miss and D. Reed); Grand Isle Residence (Lake Champlain, Vermont, 1988-91 (with D. Reed), Garden, Richmond, Massachusetts, 1989 (with D. Reed and T. Mitani); Family Cemetery, Troy, Ohio, 1990 (with D. Reed), Esplanade Roof Terrace, Cambridge, Massachusetts, 1991 (with D. Reed and T. Mitani); Nantucket Island Residence, Massachusetts, 1992 (with D. Reed); Belvedere Park, Battery Park, New York, 1995, Carl Shapiro, Beth Israel Hospital, Boston, Massachusetts, 1996 (with D. Reed), Seaside Garden, Gloucester, Massachusetts, Vassar Street, with Cambridge, Master plan, New York Botanical Gardens Garden & New Visitor, Cornell University's Ornithology Laboratory, Ithaca. **Selected bibliography** M. van Valkenburgh, *Transforming the American Garden,* Cambridge, 1986; M. Treib, *Modern Landscape Architecture: A Critical Review,* Cambridge, 1993; I. L. McHarg, *Design with Nature,* New York, 1994; G. Cooper, G. Taylor, *Paradise Transformed: The Private Garden for the Twenty-First Century,* New York, 1996; *Designed Landscape Forum 1,* edited by G. Crandell and E. Reitelss, Washington, 1998; A. Berrizbeitia, L. Pollak, *Inside Outside: Between Architecture and Landscape,* Gloucester (Mass.), 1999; *100 Years of Landscape Architecture: Some Patterns of a Century,* edited by M. Simo, Washington, 1999.

Family Cemetery,
Troy, Ohio, 1990.

Beth Israel Hospital,
Boston, 1996
(Steve Rosenthal Photo).

South Cove, Battery
Park City, New York, 1988
(Cymie Payne Photo).

CHRISTO & JEANNE-CLAUDE

Christo
& Jeanne-Claude

Bulgaria, 1935
Morocco, 1935

Among the most famous interpreters of Land Art, Christo and Jeanne-Claude in the sixties began devoting their attention to creating a new relationship between artist and landscape. Their work does not particularly tend to alter the site in which they intervene, instead they prefer to conceal, to hide, to separate places or elements that can disappear without altering their identity. So bright-coloured parasols are scattered over vast areas, canvasses wrap islands, buildings or create boundaries and trajectories, like curtains lowered and stretched between two mountains. Furthermore, in the choice of materials special attention is paid to the demanding dimensions of the installation, whose duration always seems temporary. Unlike other artists of Land Art, the sites they choose are not just indifferent ones offered by American nature, but also city sites like bridges, statues, entire buildings that are transformed, creating new, entirely unforeseen spaces.

16

Valley Curtain,
Grand Hogback,
Colorado, 1970–72
(Harry Shunk Photo).

Wrapped Trees,
Fondation Beyeler
and Berower Park,
Riehen, Switzerland,
1997–98.

Wrapped Walkways,
Jacob Loose Park,
Kansas City,
Missouri, 1977–78
(Wolfgang Volz Photo).

Works (a selection) Running Fence, Sonoma and Marin Counties, California, 1972–76: nylon woven fabric curtain 5.5 metres high, over 39.4 kms long, over 200,000 square metres of fabric and 145 kms of steel cables and 2050 steel supporting poles; Wrapped Walkways, Jacob Loose Park, Kansas City, Missouri, 1977–78: 12,500 square metres of nylon woven fabric covering over 4.5 kms of the park avenues and paths; Surrounded Islands, Biscayne Bay, Greater Miami, Florida: 603,850 square metres of woven pink polypropylene fabric, 1980–83; The Umbrellas, Japan-Usa: 1340 blue parasols at Ibaraki, Japan and 1760 yellow parasols in California, 1984–91; Wrapped Floors and Stairways and Covered Windows, Museum Würth, Künzelsau, Germany, 1995; Wrapped Reichstag, Berlin, 1995: 100,000 square metres of fabric, 5600 metres of rope, 200 tons of steel; Wrapped Trees, Fondation Beyeler, Berower Park, Riehen-Basel, Switzerland, 1997–98: 178 trees, 55,000 square metres of fabric and 23 kms of rope; Wrapped Floors and Stairways and Covered Windows, Fondazione Palazzo Bricherasio, Turin, 1998; The Wall, 13,000,011 Barrels, Gasometer, Oberhausen, Germany: indoors installation, 1999. **Selected bibliography** Christo: Works 1958–83, Tokyo, 1984; Christo, Paris-New York, 1985; Christo: Prints and Objects, 1963–1987, edited by J. Schellmann and J. Benecke, Munich-New York, 1988; Christo, edited by M. Vaizey, Barcelona-New York-Paris-Amsterdam-Tokyo, 1990; Christo. Obra 1958–1991, Barcelona, 1991; Christo and Jeanne-Claude: Prints and Objects. Catalogue Raisonné 1963–95, Munich, 1995; Christo, Jeanne-Claude, Erreurs Les Plus Fréquentes, Paris, 1998; Jeanne-Claude, M. Yanagi, Christo and Jeanne-Claude, The Umbrellas, Japan-Usa, 1984–1991, Cologne, 1998; K. Ganser, M. Taube, D. Bourdon, Christo and Jeanne-Claude, Gasometer Oberhausen, Cologne, 1999.

Wrapped Coast,
Little Bay,
Sydney, 1968–69
(Harry Shunk Photo).

Surrounded Islands,
Biscayne Bay, Greater
Miami, Florida, 1980–83
(Wolfgang Volz Photo).

Running Fence, Sonoma
and Marin Counties,
California, 1972–76
(Jeanne-Claude Photo).

Gilles Clément

France
1943

An unusual figure among French landscape architects, he started his career making private gardens, reflecting on the idea of the garden in connection with the present notions of scientific knowledge, especially biology, rather than calling upon historical or aesthetic models. In the eighties he developed the theory of the "shifting garden"—wastelands that are gradually turned into gardens by the careful introduction of new essences and where the plants follow their own biological rhythms—a theory tried out in various projects and successfully displayed in Paris at the Parc André Citroën, where he worked with Patrick Berger. Again in Paris his Serial Gardens become autonomous landscape units, where the plants determine the arrangement of the space and organize the landscape. So the garden, by a sophisticated use of the biological and aesthetic characteristics of the various essences, retrieves its complex culture and distinction. Clément materialized his ecological and didactic commitment, among other things, in mounting the exhibition "Le jardin planétaire" (The Planetary Garden), where he combined in a single perspective landscape and ecology, considering each fragment to be an intrinsic part of that vaster garden, our planet.

Parc André Citroën,
Paris, 1989–92
(Olivo Barbieri Photo).

Works Père-Lachaise Cemetery, Paris; Parc de Bercy, Paris; Park of the Château de Bénouville, Provence, France, 1987; Domaine du Rayol, Provence, France, 1988–97; Parc André Citroën, Paris, 1989–92; Garden of the Grande Arche at La Défense, Paris, 1991–97; Parc Henri Matisse, Lille, France, 1992–97; Environmental arrangement of the Lausanne-Ochy underground circuit, Lausanne, 1997; Wood of Villa Medici, Rome, 2000. **Selected bibliography** G. Clément, *Le Jardin en mouvement. De la Vallée au Parc André Citroën*, Paris, 1994; G. Clément, *Eloge de la Friche*, Paris, 1994; G. Clément, M. Blazy, *Contribution à l'étude du jardin planétaire*, Valence, 1995; G. Clément, *Une école buissonnière*, Paris, 1997; G. Clément, *Les Libres Jardins*, Paris, 1997; G. Clément, *Thomas le voyageur*, Paris, 1997; *Les Libres Jardins de G. Clément*, Paris, 1997; *World of Environmental Design*, edited by F. Asensio Cerver, Barcelona, 1998; G. Clément, *Les portes*, Paris, 1998; M. Hucliez, *Jardins et parcs contemporains*, Paris, 1999; G. Clément, *Le Jardin planétaire*, Paris, 1999; I. Cortesi, *Il parco pubblico. Paesaggi 1985–2000*, Milan, 2000. His works are published in the reviews *Arca, Architects' Journal, Architecture Today, D'Architectures, Landscape Architecture, Landscape Australia, L'Architecture d'aujourd'hui, Lotus international, Lotus navigator, Monuments Historiques, Pages Paysages, Progressive Architecture, Techniques & Architecture.*

limited by the boundaries of the biosphere,

then it is exactly in the same situation as the garden:

a closed, autonomous and fragile environment
where every element interferes with the whole
and the whole acts upon every being"

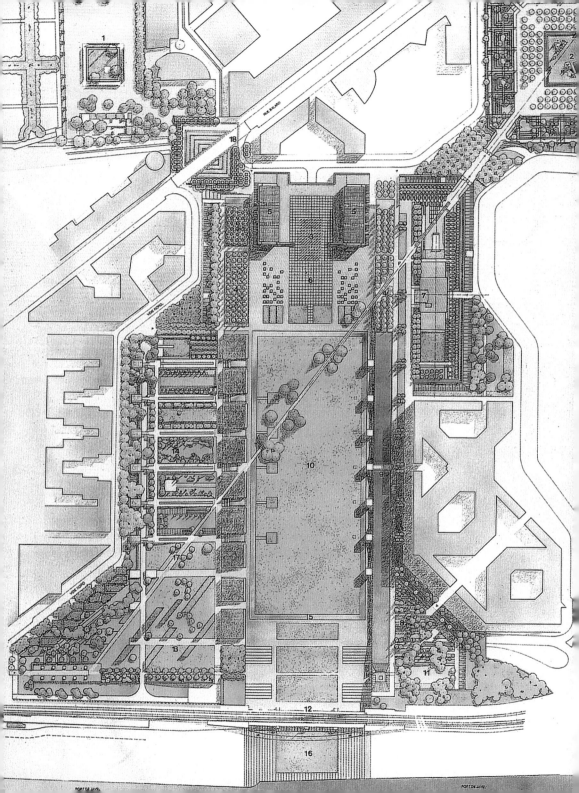

Parc André Citroën,
Paris, 1989–92
(Olivo Barbieri Photos)

"The wasteland becomes tane, nature educated,
even if the taning should always
come about gently"

Michel Corajoud

France

1937

He is one of the masters of contemporary French landscape architecture; his designs for city parks always display special care for the environmental and architectural features already present in the site. In the Parc du Sausset, Corajoud draws from the entire landscape and architecture culture, designing new patterns and availing himself of the particular morphology to create diversified ecosystems, selecting the essences not merely according to aesthetic standards. The various units of the landscape, determined by the vacant spaces of the clearings, the pattern of the axes, the rows of trees and the morphological links, and enhanced by the waters of the Sausset, arrange the park in keeping with its three main uses: the forest, in the French tradition, the city park and the *bocage*. His art is also indebted to his special concern for the transformations of the essences in time and his ability to incorporate everything that already forms the landscape, including motorways, electric and railroad lines, buildings and works of art. He has worked for a number of years with Claire Corajoud, and teaches at Versailles, where in 1977 he was partly responsible for turning the Ecole Nationale d'Horticulture into the Ecole Nationale Supérieure du Paysage.

Parc du Sausset,
Villepinte, Seine-Saint-Denis,
Aulnay-sous-Bois, 1994
(Gérard Dufresne Photo).

Works Parc des Coudrays, Maurepas Elancourt, France, 1974; Parc de la Villeneuve, Grenoble, France, 1974; Parc du Sausset, Villepinte, Seine-Saint-Denis, Aulnay-sous-Bois, France, 1981–94; Parc de la Tête d'Or, Lyon, France, 1990–93 (with R. Piano); Plaine Saint-Denis Hippodamos 93, Saint-Denis, France, 1990–99 (with Y. Lion, P. Roboulet, P. Robert); Quay and Boulevard Charles de Gaulle, Lyon, France, 1993–97; Wilson Gardens, Plaine Saint-Denis, 1994–98; Avenue d'Italie, Paris, 1995–98; Boulevard Tony Garnier, Lyon, France, 1999–2000; Parc de Gerland, Lyon, France, 1999–2005; Parc de la Trinité, Saint-Denis, France, 1999–. **Selected bibliography** A. Roger, *La Théorie du paysage en France, 1974–1994*, Champ Vallon, 1995; M. Hucliez, *Jardins et parcs contemporains*, Paris, 1999; G. Donin, *Parchi/Parks*, Cannitello (Villa San Giovanni, Italy), 1999; I. Cortesi, *Il parco pubblico. Paesaggi 1985–2000*, Milan, 2000. His projects and theoretic writings have been published in the reviews *Arquitectura Viva, Bauwelt, Casabella, Connaissance des arts, Garten und Landschaft, Japan Landscape, Korean Landscape Architecture, Landskab, L'Architecture d'aujourd'hui, Le Moniteur Architecture, Techniques & Architecture, Topos*.

*Covering
for Motorway A1,*
Saint-Denis, 1998.

Parc du Sausset,
Villepinte, Seine-Saint-Denis,
Aulnay-sous-Bois, 1994
(Gérard Dufresne Photo).

CHARLES CORREA

Charles Correa

India

1930

An architect and urbanist, a rather unusual personality compared to the more well-known contemporary landscapers. In the gardens of his works, for instance in the Jawahar Kala Kendra and the campus of the University of Pune, Correa succeeds in mingling powerful mementos of Indian tradition with modernism, especially in his return to the original conception of architecture as reflection of the cosmos and of nature and, as such, a way to express the most essential, profound concepts of present-day society. At Pune the walls, reflecting the colour of space, recapture the vision of the universe expanding out of a central vortex—a stone *kund*—and the open spaces are connotated by kinetic forms or elements expressing ancient symbology. A pioneer in low-cost building in the Third World, from 1970 to 1975 he was director of the Planning Commission for New Bombay. In 1985 he was appointed president of the national Urbanism Commission; he taught in several universities including, in the United States, the Massachusetts Institute of Technology, and at Cambridge.

IUCAA, Pune, 1992.

Jawahar Kala Kendra, Jaipur, 1992.

Works (a selection) Mahatma Gandhi Memorial, Ahmedabad, 1958–63; Kanchanjunga Palace, Bombay, 1970–83; Bharat Bhavan Museum, Bhopal, 1975–81; Sabarmati Ashram State Assembly, Madhya Pradesh; Jawahar Kala Kendra, Jaipur, India, 1986–92; IUCAA, Pune, India, 1988–92.
Selected bibliography *Charles Correa: Form Follows Climate*, London, 1980; *Architecture in the Seventies*, edited by U. Kultermann, London, 1980; *Charles Correa*, Singapore, 1983; C. Correa, *The New Landscape*, Bombay, 1985 (New York, 1989); *Charles Correa*, edited by Hasan-Uddin Khan, Singapore-London-New York, 1987; *Modern Architecture*, edited by W. R. Curtis, London, 1987; *Contemporary Architecture*, Chicago-London, 1987; *A History of Architecture*, edited by B. Fletcher, London, 1987; *100 Contemporary Architects: Drawings & Sketches*, edited by B. Lacy, London, 1991; *Modern Architecture: A Critical History*, edited by K. Frampton, London, 1992; *The Architecture of the Jumping Universe*, edited by C. Jencks, London, 1995; *Contemporary Asian Architects*, edited by Hasan-Uddin Khan, Koln-London-New York, 1995; *The Tropical Asian House*, edited by R. Powell, Singapore, 1996; *Architecture After Modernism*, edited by D. Ghirardo, London, 1996; *Contemporary Vernacular*, edited by W. Lim and Tan Hock Beng, Singapore, 1997; *Charles Correa*, edited by C. Correa, K. Frampton and H. Correa, London, 1997; *Outside Architecture*, edited by S. Zevon, London-Gloucester-Cincinnati, 1999; C. Correa, *Housing & Urbanisation / Charles Correa*, London, 2000.

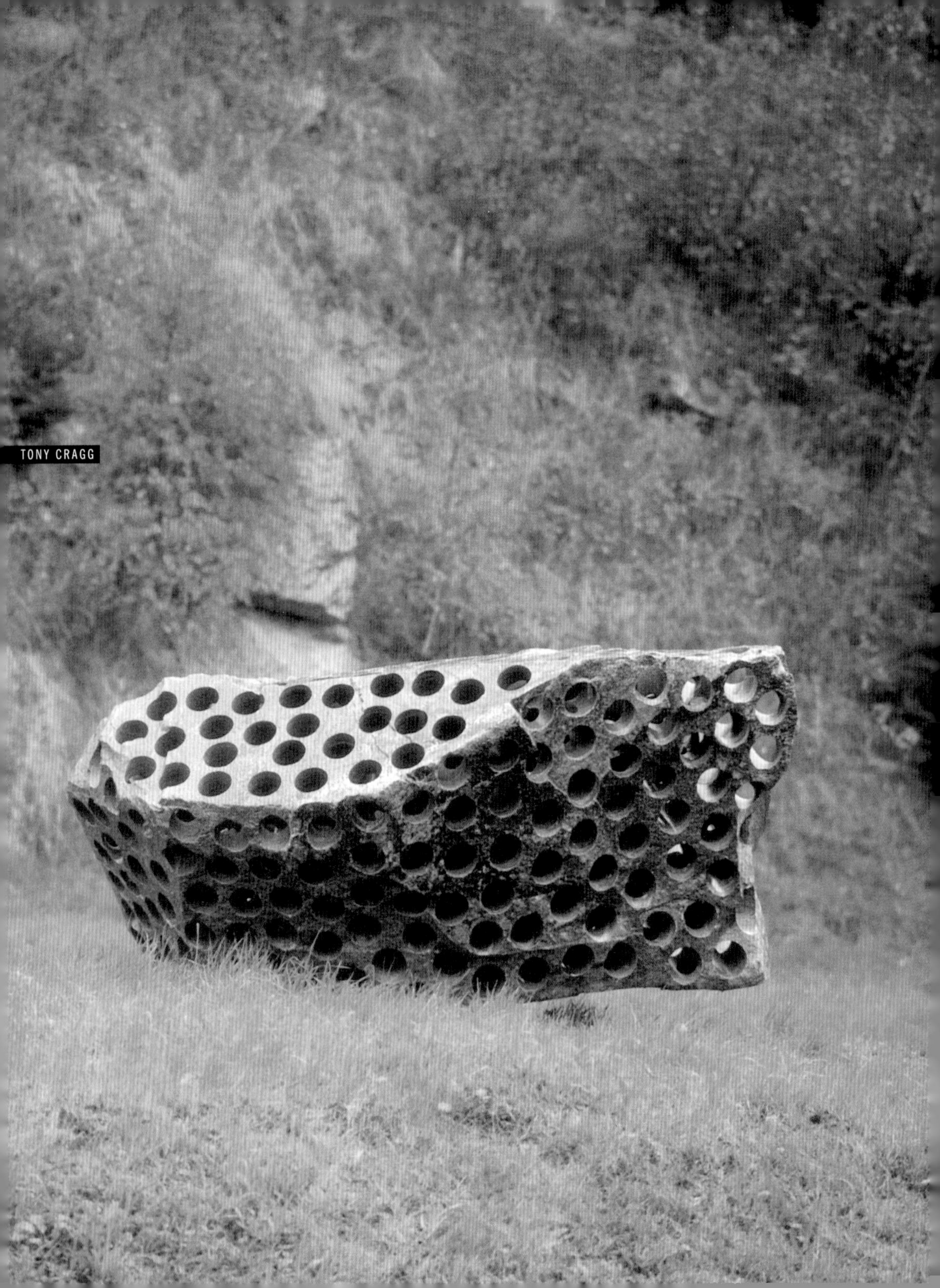

Tony Cragg

Great Britain

1949

Tony Cragg was trained at the Royal Academy of Arts in London, and in the eighties, with Anish Kapoor and Richard Deacon, was acclaimed as one of the protagonists of new English sculpture. In the industrial area of the Ruhr in Germany he created sculptures out of discarded material, in particular wood and plastic. City trash—plates, bottles, cans, toys—was selected and arranged according to colour and shape, creating post-industrial rainbows, or else laid out like tesserae to form images. In his latest works, Cragg extended his range of materials—always emphasizing their sculptural vocation—working on pieces based on the use of a single material. "Thus we have castings in bronze, iron, ceramic and glass. Images of alembics and laboratory test tubes, enlarged and almost anthropomorphic, recur frequently in his iconography, along with recreated landscapes of contemporary archaeology. An extremely prolific artist, Cragg literally succeeds in reaching and glorifying the essence and the possibilities of the materials he uses, almost revealing their hidden molecular structure."

20

100 Spear, 1990.

Re-Forming, 1992.

Exhibitions "Britannica: Vingt-cinq ans de sculpture", Le Havre, France, 1988; Biennale di Venezia, Venice, 1988; Kunstammlung Nordrhein Westfalen, Düsseldorf, 1989; Tate Gallery, London, 1989; Stedelijk van Abbe Museum, Eindhoven, 1989; "Magiciens de la Terre", Paris, 1989; Museum of Art, Tel Aviv, 1990; Newport Harbour Art Museum, California, 1990–92; Wiener Secession, Vienna, 1991; IVAM Centro Julio Gonzáles, Valencia, 1992; CCA, Glasgow, 1992; Kunsthalle, Vienna, 1993; Musée des Beaux-Arts, Nantes, 1994; Stadtgalerie, Saarbrücken, 1994; Kunstverein, St. Gallen, 1994; Museo Nacional Centro de Arte Reina Sofía, Madrid, 1995; Centre Georges Pompidou, Paris, 1996. **Selected bibliography** *Tony Cragg: Eine Werkauswahl* (Galerie Buchmann), Basel, 1990; *Tony Cragg. Sculpture 1975–1990* (Newport Harbor Art Museum), New York, 1991; *Tony Cragg* (Wiener Secession), Vienna, 1991; T. Cragg, *Ecrits/Writings/Geschriften*, Brussels, 1992; *Tony Cragg* (Trento, Galleria Civica di Arte Contemporanea), Milan, 1994; *Anthony Cragg* (Madrid, Museo Nacional Centro de Arte Reina Sofía), Madrid, 1995; *Tony Cragg* (Paris, Musée National d'Art Moderne, Centre Georges Pompidou), 1996; G. Célant, *Cragg*, Milan-London, 1996; *Tony Cragg: Sculpture* (London, Whitechapel Art Gallery), 1997.

DE

TOPHER DELANEY

Topher Delaney

Usa

Investigating the cultural symbols inherent to the development of a site, and interpreting perceptions of reality—in collaboration with future users—are the thematic guidelines the T. Delaney Inc. studio follows in creating countless gardens and parks for civic, health, educational or religious institutions. Among the latest designs illustrating this commitment we should mention the park-garden at the San Diego Children's Hospital: you enter through the skeleton of a dinosaur wrapped in bougainvillea, and can admire fountains shaped like sea horses, sky-blue walls, lush plantations of medicinal herbs and a windmill; Fox Creek Park at Contra Costa Center, where the walkways cross a stream that has been rehabilitated as a dynamic biome; in New York the Inn of the Beth Israel Hospital, a terrace of sculptures for children with neurological problems; a meditation garden, formed of rocks and water, for a Buddhist community; a sculpture garden at Greenwich, surrounded by trapezoidal, arched shapes made of stainless steel, concrete and granite; a design for urban space, in San Francisco, that integrates a plantation of sunflowers with a major transportation artery.

Oliver Garden,
San Francisco,
California.

*Data Center
Roof Garden*,
Bank of America,
San Francisco,
California, 1994.

*San Diego
Children's Hospital*,
San Diego,
California, 1997.

Works (a selection) Sculpture Garden for the Portland Art Museum; Highland Learning Museum for the Highland Hospital of Oakland, California; Milstein Residence, Greenwich, Connecticut, 1992–93; Marin Cancer Institute Healing Garden, Marin General Hospital, Greenbrae, California, 1993; Kuhling Garden, Palo Alto, California, Usa, 1993; Data Center Roof Garden, Bank of America, San Francisco, California, 1993–94; Pemberton Grade, San Francisco, California; Inn of the Beth Israel Hospital, New York; The Leichtag Family Healing Garden, San Diego Children's Hospital, San Diego, California, 1997; Fox Creek Park, Contra Costa Center. **Selected bibliography** G. Cooper, G. Taylor, *Paradise Transformed. The Private Garden for the Twenty-First Century*, New York, 1996; G. Cooper, G. Taylor, *Gardens for the Future*, New York, 2000; M. Leccese, *American Eden. Landscape Architecture of the Pacific West*, Paris, 2000.

"Gardens should be freed
from the boxwood of history"

WALTER DE MARIA

Walter De Maria

Usa

1935

The *Lightning Field* Walter De Maria created from 1971 to 1977 on a desert plateau in New Mexico, at an altitude of approximately one thousand metres, is one of the most celebrated examples of Minimal Art and just a part of this artist's work: over a surface of about 25,000 square metres, a few hundred stainless steel rods, six metres tall, are placed at regular intervals and aligned. Like a mirror, they reflect and measure solar light at the different times of the day, and create spectacular effects by attracting lightning produced by the frequent storms. Invisible from afar, the symbolic presence of these pieces—that generate light, even if only reflected, in the daytime—is not perceived until you are inside the installation. De Maria's great meteorological arrangement is a perfectly automated ecological machine, where the human being is turned into an observer and consumer of a specially recreated spectacular nature. Shared by other Land Art artists, De Maria's idea is to "build the place" in the only place in nature that is still "natural": the desert.

Lightning Field,
Quemado, New Mexico,
1971–77.

Works (a selection) Boxes for Meaningless Work, 1961; Las Vegas Piece, Desert Valley, Nevada, 1969; Desert Cross, El Mirage Dry Lake, Nevada, 1969; Lightning Field, Quemado, New Mexico, 1971–77; The New York Earth Room, Dia Center for the Arts, New York, 1977; Vertical Earth Kilometer, Friedrichsplatz, Kassel, 1977. **Exhibitions** Documenta IV, Kassel, 1968; Documenta VI, Kassel, 1977; " Sculpture Nature", Villerbanne, France, 1980; "Walter De Maria", Centre Georges Pompidou, Paris, 1981; "More or Less. Pop Art and Minimalism", Malmö, Sweden, 1995; "Walter De Maria. The 2000 Sculpture", Kunsthaus, Zurich, 2000. **Selected bibliography** G. and S. Jellicoe, *The Landscape of Man*, London, 1975; L. R. Lippard, *Overlay*, New York, 1983; J. Brown, *The English Garden in Our Time*, Suffolk, 1986; K. Baker, *Minimalism*, New York, 1988; J. Beardsley, *Earthworks and Beyond*, New York, 1989; G. A. Tiberghien, *Land Art*, New York-Paris, 1995; *Land and Environmental Art*, edited by J. Kastner and B. Wallis, Hong Kong, 1998.

Georges Descombes

Switzerland
1939

Public park,
Lancy, Geneva, 1986.

La Voie Suisse,
Uri, 1990.

In the park of Lancy, on the edge of Geneva, in a blurred, blighted territory, a few marginal elements, an apparent austerity toward figures and context and an awareness of the traces the site had preserved, have recreated a geography of correspondences with what was there before, and given rise to a specific place. The conceptual themes of the relationship between architecture and landscape and "going through", recurrent in Descombes' work, also can be seen in La Voie Suisse, a physical and conceptual park-circuit that winds its way over 35 kilometres around the Uri Lake. He taught at the Berlage Institute of Amsterdam, the Graduate School of Design at Harvard, the School of Architecture of the University of Virginia and the Ecole de Versailles; presently he teaches at the Architecture Institute of the University of Geneva.

Works Public park at Lancy, Geneva, 1980–86; La Voie Suisse, Uri, Switzerland, 1987–90; Promenade St. Antoine, Geneva, 1992–94; Westwijkplein, Amsterdam, 1992–94; Lustgarten, Berlin, 1994; Bijlmermeer Park Monument, Amsterdam, 1994–98; De Grote Rietplas, Emmen, Netherlands, 1996; Public park, Freiburg, Switzerland, 1999–; Rue la Corraterie, Geneva, 2000–. **Selected bibliography** G. Descombes, "La moindre des choses", in *Herman Hertzberger. Six architectures photographiées par Johan van der Keuken*, Milan, 1985; *Georges Descombes: il territorio transitivo*, edited by G. Tironi, Rome, 1988; A. Léveillé, G. Descombes, *Voie suisse: l'itinéraire genevois*, Geneva, 1991; *Denatured Visions. Landscape and Culture in the Twentieth Century*, edited by S. Wrede and W. H. Adams, New York, 1991; J. Corner, *Recovering Landscape*, Princeton, 1999; I. Cortesi, *Il parco pubblico. Paesaggi 1985–2000*, Milan, 2000. His projects are published in the reviews *Abitare, Anthos, Archis, Architect, Bauen + Wohnen, Casabella, Domus, L'Architecture d'aujourd'hui, Parametro, Passages, Spazio e Società, Werk.*

DESVIGNE & DALNOKY

Michel Desvigne
& Christine Dalnoky

France
1958 and 1956

For Desvigne and Dalnoky making gardens is a discipline that does not aim at imitating nature (yet while not seeking merely decorative results), and whereby they can conceive a series of devices that reproduce, enlarging them, the very natural forms they refuse to imitate. At Issoudun their concern for the place's specific features led the two authors to regularize the design grid by the usual system of breaking up the territory into plots of land, which becomes once again the method for putting order in spaces and circuits, avoiding any attempt to restore and preserve the old traces and structures of a landscape where the activities have changed. At Guyancourt the presence of an industrial plant and an indifferent background is not a hindrance, but makes it possible to create a work connected with agricultural cycles and arranged in a series of stages that imply a constant transformation of the plantations, even once the factory is closed down. At Lyon, a public plaza becomes a secret, protective place: a raised wooden platform you can walk on, surrounded by thick magnolia and rhododendron foliage, suggesting a living-room.

24

City Park,
Issoudun, Indre, 1997.

Works Outdoor Spaces of the Thompson Manufacture, Guyancourt, France, 1988–92; Garden Rue de Meaux, Paris, 1990; Place des Célestins, Lyon, France, 1991; Area of Port Marianne, Montpellier, France, 1991–2000; City Park, Issoudun, Indre, France, 1994–97; Landscape TGV Station, Avignon, Marseilles, 1995–98; Marianne Park, Montpellier, France, 1996–; Access to the Airport of Roissy-Charles de Gaulle, Paris, 1996–2000; Viaduct of Avignon, Vaucluse, France, 1998–2000; Millennium Park, Greenwich, London, 1998–2000; Outdoor Spaces Zac Alésia Montsouris, Paris; Marine Park, Trieste, Italy; Barcelona Viaduct of Millau; Colline de Fourvière, Lyon, France; Middelheim Sculpture Park, Antwerp, Belgium, 1999; Centraal Museum Garden, Utrecht, Netherlands, 1999; Park for the Fort Thüngen Museum of Modern Art, Luxemburg, 2000. **Selected bibliography** G. A. Tiberghien, *Michel Desvigne: Jardins élémentaires*, Rome, 1988; *The Landscape. Four International Landscape Designers: Hargreaves Associates, Desvigne & Dalnoky, West 8 Landscape Architects, Lapeña & Torres*, Antwerp, 1995; *Desvigne & Dalnoky*, Milan, 1996; *Desvigne & Dalnoky. The Return of the Landscape*, New York, 1997; M. Hucliez, *Jardins et parcs contemporains*, Paris, 1999; I. Cortesi, *Il parco pubblico. Paesaggi 1985–2000*, Milan, 2000; *Anthos, Architect, Architectural Review, Arquitectura Viva, Bauwelt, Casabella, Domus, Landscape Architecture, L'Architecture d'aujourd'hui, Le Moniteur Architecture, Lotus international, Metropolis, Techniques & Architecture, Topos.*

*Park for the Fort Thüngen
Museum of Modern Art,*
Luxemburg, 2000.

City Park,
Issoudun, Indre, 1997.

F

FERRATER, CANOSA, FIGUERAS

Carlos Ferrater
José Luis Canosa
Bet Figueras

Spain

Botanical Garden,
Montjuic, Barcelona, 1999.

Mostly known for their lengthy sequence of architectural projects, Carlos Ferrater, José Luis Canosa and Bet Figueras have recently completed the design for the Botanical Garden in Barcelona, the very latest intervention on the Montjuic following the Palau Sant Jordi by Arata Isozaki, Calatrava's communications tower and the stadium remodelled by Gregotti, Milá and Correa. The garden does not display the usual series of floral patterns, as in a phyto-botanical collection, but strives to unify the theme in a single approach. A triangular grid serves as geometric background for the layout of the fifteen hectares of garden and to delineate circuits following the contour lines best suited to the present topography. So the area is broken up in a number of units, separate and fragmented—just like the plant varieties of the Earth— that present the species in a phyto-geographic type of botanical circuit.

Works Botanical Garden, Barcelona, 1999. **Selected bibliography** *AV Monographs*, 79-80, 1999. *AV Monograph*, 81-82, 2000.

Caminho
das Gaivotas

Estacada
das Gaivotas

João Nunes Ferreira

Portugal
1960

Parque do Tejo e Trancão,
Lisbon, 1998.

Trained in Lisbon and at the Escuela Técnica Superior de Arquitectura in Barcelona, in 1986 Nunes Ferreira worked as a landscaper for the City of Lisbon, and in 1989 founded Proap, a landscape architecture studio. With George Hargreaves he designed the new Parque do Tejo e Trancão in Lisbon for Expo '98, in which the huge area where the two rivers meet was rehabilitated for various activities like sports, environmental education, leisure and relaxation. The design seems to combine ecological ethics—represented by the permanence of the place's original features—with a sculptural handling of the surfaces, justified by functional as well as symbolic factors. Lately he has created two other major parks: the Jardim Almirante Reis, at Madeira, between the old walls and the sea at Funchal, and the city park of Quinta de Politeira in Lisbon where he remodelled an old farm.

Works Parque do Tejo e Trancão, Lisbon, 1998 (with Hargreaves Associates); Park, Funchal, Madeira, Portugal; Park of Quinta de Politeira, Lisbon, 1998-2000. **Selected bibliography** L. Vassalo Rosa, "A urbanização da zona de intervenção", in *Lisboa Expo '98*, Lisbon, 1998, pp. 38-40; I. Cortesi, *Il parco pubblico. Paesaggi 1985-2000*, Milan, 2000; *Landscape Design, Lotus international, Process Architecture.*

Ian Hamilton Finlay

Great Britain
[Bahamas]

1925

Little Sparta,
Stonypath,
Lanarkshire, Scotland
(A. Lawson Photo).

Poet and gardener. In phase with American Earth Art, in 1974 in Scotland, at Stonypath, Hamilton Finlay turned a moor into a succession of gardens that feature inscriptions referring to the landscape tradition in art, literature and history; together with the countless bits of architecture scattered about the garden, they create a series of conceptual and philosophical places. This "concrete poetry" that explored materials and environment at Stonypath has turned out to be an entirely new model of mediation with the world we live in. Finlay's importance, years later, seems quite remarkable: "No poet", Stephen Bann writes, "has gone further in investing the natural world with philosophical importance, by attaching himself to the classical tradition in general and the English tradition of the poet-gardener in particular."

Permanent works Garden of the Max Planck Institut, Stuttgart, 1975; Scottish National Gallery of Modern Art, Royal Botanic Garden, Edinburgh, 1975; University of Liège, Belgium, 1976; Bell's Garden, Perth, Scotland, 1978; British Embassy, Bonn, 1979; Kröller-Müller Sculpture Garden, Otterlo, Netherlands, 1982; Garden of Giuliano Gori, Celle, Italy, 1984; Schweizergarten, Vienna, 1986; Stedelijk van Abbe Museum, Eindhoven, Netherlands, 1986; Skulptur Projekt, Münster, 1987; Campus of the University of California, San Diego, 1987; Furka Pass, Switzerland, 1987; West Princes Street Gardens, Edinburgh, 1987; Museum of Modern Art, Strasbourg, 1988; Harris Museum and Art Gallery, Preston, England, 1988; Private library of Ungers, Cologne, 1989; 12th & K Office Tower, Sacramento, California, 1990; Railway Bridge, Glasgow, 1990; Stockwood Park Nurseries in the Borough of Luton, England, 1991; Library of Baden, Karlsruhe, 1991; Overbeck, Gesellschaft, Lubeck, 1991; Shenstone's Leasowes, Dudley, England, 1992; Floriadepark, Zoetermeer, Netherlands, 1992; Beelden op de Berg, Belmonte Arboretum, Wageningen, Netherlands, 1993; Laumeier Sculpture Park, St. Louis, 1994; Schröder Münchmeyer Hengst & Co. Bank, Frankfurt am Main, 1994; The Gyle, Shopping Centre, Edinburgh, 1994; Landesgartenschau, Grevenbroich, Germany, 1995; Botanic Garden of the University of Durham, England, 1996; Hunter Square, Edinburgh, 1997; Kunsthalle, Hamburg, 1997; Serpentine Gallery, London, 1998; The Ark, London, 1998; Bundesarbeitsgericht, Erfurt, Germany, 1999; BUGA, Magdeburg, Germany, 1999; Park am Goetheturm/GrünGürtel, Frankfurt am Main, 1999; Bundesanwaltschaft, Karlsruhe, 1999; Island of La Xunqueira del Lérez, Pontevedra, Spain, 1999; Poetry Library, Edinburgh, 2000; Hamilton, Scotland, 2000; Wallraff-Richartz-Museum, Cologne, 2000; Monastery of Schönthal, Switzerland, 2000; Patumbah Park, Zurich, 2000. **Selected bibliography** D. Boudinetin, *Un paysage ou 9 vues du jardin de Ian Hamilton Finlay*, Jouy-en-Josas, 1987; *Wood Notes Wild: Essays on the Poetry and Art of Ian Hamilton Finlay*, Edinburgh, 1995; F. Zdenek, P. Simig, *Ian Hamilton Finlay: Works in Europe 1972–1995*, Ostfildern, 1995; G. Cooper, G. Taylor, *Paradise Transformed. The Private Garden for the Twenty-First Century*, New York, 1996; *Rubber Stamps from the Little Spartan War*, Morning Star Publications, 1997; *Prints 1963–1997 Druckgrafik*, edited by R. E. Pahlke and P. Simig, Cantz, 1997; R. Gillanders, *Little Sparta. A Portrait of a Garden*, National Galleries of Scotland, 1998; *Land and Environmental Art*, edited by J. Kastner and B. Wallis, Hong Kong, 1998; I. Cortesi, *Il parco pubblico. Paesaggi 1985–2000*, Milan, 2000.

"Gardening activity is of five kinds,

namely, sowing, planting, fixing,

placing, maintaining.

In so far as gardening is an art,

all these may be taken under the one head,

composing"

SHADOW n. the hour-hand

See over there – the rooftops of
the farms are already putting
up their evening smoke and
SHADOWS of the mountain
crests are falling further out

VIRGIL : ECLOGUES

G

Adriaan Geuze

Netherlands

1960

Departing from the prevailing trends in contemporary Dutch architecture and town planning, Adriaan Geuze develops landscape design in a new, original fashion. All his works—that deal with every field connected with the design and treatment of public areas—display his ability to associate town planning issues, the experience of contemporary art and the handling of facilities. They represent a design and operational model that has been a turning point in our way of thinking about the landscape and transforming it. In the Schouwburgplein of Rotterdam, the main plaza of the city, he uses wooden and metal grid paving and imposing mobile structures for lighting to create a formally defined space, with a wealth of urban connections. At Tilburg, where cultural references have little to do with the history of the city and the tradition of the art of gardens, he borrows expressions drawn from the pictorial artistic avant-gardes. In 1987 he founded the West 8 Landscape Architect studio that groups architects, town planners, designers and landscapers from all over the world.

Schouwburgplein,
Rotterdam, 1990–97.

Schipol Airport landscape,
Amsterdam.

Works (a selection) Schipol Airport Landscape, Amsterdam; Carrasco Square, Amsterdam; Schouwburgplein, Rotterdam, Netherlands, 1990–97; Teleport Park, Amsterdam, 1992–96; VBS Garden, Rijnsweerd, Utrecht, Netherlands, 1994–95; Cypress Swamp Garden, Spoleto Festival, Italy, 1997; Interpolis Garden, Tilburg, Netherlands, 1997–98; "Des os et des citrouilles", Chaumont-sur-Loire, France, 2000. **Selected bibliography** *Adriaan Geuze/West 8: Landscape Architecture,* Rotterdam, 1995; A. Geuze, *In Holland staat een huis,* Rotterdam, 1995; U. Weilacher, *Between Landscape Architecture and Land Art,* Berlin-Basel-Boston, 1996; J. Beardsley, *Art and Landscape. In Charleston and the Low Country,* Washington, 1998; I. Cortesi, *Il parco pubblico. Paesaggi 1985–2000,* Milan, 2000; *A+U, Archis, Architect, Architectural Record, Arquitectura Viva, Blueprint, Building Design, Casabella, Daidalos, De Architect Domus, Landskab, L'Architecture d'aujourd'hui, Lotus international, Quaderns d'arquitectura i urbanisme, Ville e Giardini, World Architecture, 2G.*

Cypress Swamp Garden,
Moncks Corner,
Charleston, 1997.

Des os et des citrouilles,
Chaumont-sur-Loire, 2000.

Interpolis Garden,
Tilburg, 1997-98.

Christophe Girot

France

1957

The concept of time in all its aspects is the central theme of his work, featuring forceful, simple gestures performed in the landscape. Indeed, in his most important designs we can make out his intent to transform these gestures in the framework of the various human activities and the natural evolutions of time. Yet his gardens are always "slow" places, simple and refreshing, because conceived on the rhythm of the biological clock. In Berlin, in the Invaliden Park, Girot either uses the favorite motifs of contemporary American landscaping (play on lines and stretches of different materials and colours), or else avails himself of the more distinctly European version that creates careful forms that relate to the existing fabric. In the past ten years Girot performed most of his work in Europe, especially in France and Germany. He trained as an architect, landscape architect and environmental planner at Berkeley and Davis, California, during the late seventies and the early eighties. Since then he taught Landscape Design at the Ecole de Versailles, and is presently Visiting Professor in Landscape Architecture at the ETH in Zurich.

Invaliden Park,
Berlin, 1997.

Works (a selection) Jardin Jeanne d'Arc, Paris, 1992 (with Devillers and Perrot); Festival du Jardin, Chaumont-sur-Loire, France, 1993; Parc des Six Arpents, Pierrelaye, France, 1995; Parc Saint-Serge, Angers, France, 1996 (with J.-M. L'Anton and Dusapin Leclercq); Invaliden Park, Berlin, 1997; Parc Jules Guesde, Alfortville, France, 1999; Les Grands Ateliers d'Architecture, Ile d'Abeau, France, 2000–; Industrial Landscape for Hermès/Siegl, France, 2000–. **Selected bibliography** S. Simon, *Landscape and Memory*, London, 1996; J. Corner, *Recovering Landscape*, Princeton, 1999; T. Scröder, *Contemporary European Landscape Architecture*, Berlin, 2000. He is the author of a number of essays and articles in the reviews *De Wolden, Garten und Landschaft, Landscape Architecture Magazine, Landscape Design, Les Carnets du Paysage, Pages Paysages, Recovering Landscape, Topos.*

João Gomes da Silva

Portugal
1962

For Gomes da Silva landscape design, based on the study of the natural features that make up the landscape—dimensions, reasons and origins of its form, movements of air, water, vegetation—and then of the anthropic forms that present these features and are completed by alterations, additions and constant mutations, becomes the instrument for interpreting the character of a place, also documented by these series of sedimented alterations. At Malagueira the built elements organize a park and distribute its natural features: the bridges insure the continuity of the walkways over the lines for rain water drainage, while the other outdoor spaces give the impression of having been scattered throughout the housing network. From 1986 to 1990 he worked on designing public areas at Malagueira; he taught at Evora from 1987 to 1994, was Visiting Professor in Berlin, at the Ensp of Versailles, in Girona and Barcelona. Presently he is working with Inês Norton, with whom he opened the Global Paesaggio studio in 1994.

Garden of the Higher School for Tourism,
Faro, 1997
(Sergio Mah Photo).

Malaguiera,
Evora, 1987–91.

Works Plan and project for Public Spaces, Malagueira, Evora, Portugal, 1987–91; Landscape design, Higher School of Education, Setubal, Portugal, 1991–94; Landscape plan for the Walls of the Convent of Tomar, Tomar, Portugal, 1994; Detailed plan, Vilarinho Seco, Boticas, 1994; Landscape design for the Pousada in the Monastery of St. Maria Flor da Rosa, Crato, 1994–96; Detailed plan of Public Spaces Expo '98, Lisbon, 1994–98; Gracia de Orta Gardens, Expo '98, Seville, 1994–98; Garden of the Serralves Museum of Contemporary Art, Oporto, 1996–2000; Garden of the Higher School for Tourism, Faro, Portugal, 1997; Garden and Plaza of the Church of Marco de Canavezes, Portugal, 1998; Presidential Palace Gardens, Belem, Lisbon, 1998–2000; Landscape recovery project of the Spa, Monchique, 1999. **Selected bibliography** *Bauwelt, Lotus international*.

GRUPO DE DISEÑO URBANO

Grupo de Diseño Urbano

Mario Schjetnan
José Luis Pérez
Mexico
1945 and 1947

Mario Schjetnan was the founder in 1977, with José Luis Pérez, of the Grupo de Diseño Urbano specializing in landscaping, architecture and urban design. The projects for the Parque Tezozomoc and the Parque Ecológico de Xochimilco have won worldwide acclaim, and today the Xochimilco park occupies a surface of 312 hectares, which includes an authentic ecological park, a plant and flower market, a sports centre and the lagoon, designed by following the old waterways and the Aztec farming *chinampa*. The main objective of Schjetnan's and Pérez' intervention was to recover through landscaping an historical area of great relevance, without it becoming a sentimental reminiscence of the pre-Columbian past, but a natural space that could grow in the future, heedful of the exigencies of recreation, sports and tourism, and integrated with Mexico City.

Parque Ecológico de Xochimilco, Mexico City.

Works Parque Ecológico de Xochimilco, Mexico City; Parque Histórico Culhuacán, Mexico; Parque Recreativo y Cultural Tezozomoc-Azcapotzalco, Mexico; Museo de las Culturas del Norte, Paquimé, Mexico; Parque El Cedazo, Aguascalientes, Mexico; El Camino Real, Mexico. **Selected bibliography** *Designed Landscape Forum 1*, edited by G. Crandell and E. Reifeiss, Washington, 1998; *100 Years of Landscape Architecture: Some Patterns of a Century*, edited by M. Simo, Washington, 1999; *Arquitectura del Paisaje, Arquitectura y Sociedad, Artes de Mexico, Construcción y Tecnología, Garden Design, Landscape Architecture, Lotus international, Process Architecture, Revista de Arquitectura Mexico, Techniques & Architecture, Zona Verde.*

*Parque Ecológico
de Xochimilco,*
Mexico City.

Parque El Cedazo,
Aguascalientes.

Kathryn
Gustafson

Usa
1951

Trained at the Ecole de Versailles, Kathryn Gustafson has become one of the most famous contemporary landscape architects owing to her projects for the central town plaza at Evry, the *Jardins de l'Imaginaire* at Terrasson and the garden for Shell at Rueil-Malmaison. Her garden designs play on abstract, but simple, images that refer to the history of the landscape, or to personal memories: at Evry, a "field" of water spouts reminds us of its agricultural origins; at Rueil-Malmaison she created a vast roof-garden; and in New York, in designing Ross Terrace, she was inspired by a photograph of an eclipse of the moon. At Terrasson she designed a miscellany of fragments of historic gardens, reinterpreting bits of history, culture and myth, arranged either in an abstract way or by referring to the invariable features of gardens, such as terraces and water. Thus nature is designed in its most varied states: original and wild, shaped by the needs of agriculture, and finally altered by architecture. The originality of her approach lies precisely in a balanced capacity to reach a synthesis of the cultural models of contemporary landscape and those of European tradition by exploiting plain geometric shapes and the elegant juxtaposition of carefully selected materials.

Jardins de l'Imaginaire,
Terrasson, 1996.

Works Meeting Point, Morbras, France, 1987; Plaza at Evry, France, 1989; Shell Headquarters, Rueil-Malmaison, France, 1991; Esso Headquarters, Rueil-Malmaison, France, 1992; L'Oréal Headquarters, Aulnay-sous-Bois, France, 1992; Marseilles Gateway, Marseilles, 1994; Jardins de l'Imaginaire, Terrasson, France, 1996; Western Park Gasfabriek, Amsterdam, 1997; Crystal Palace Park, London, 1997; South Coast Plaza and Pedestrian Bridge, Costa Mesa, California, 1999–; Civic Center Campus, Seattle, Washington, 1999; Ross Terrace, American Museum of Natural History, New York, 2000; Swiss Cottage Garden, London, 2000–; Garden of Forgiveness, Beirut, 2000–; Seattle Performance Hall and Theater District, Seattle, 2000–. **Selected bibliography** J. Beardsley, *Earthworks and Beyond*, New York, 1989; D. Imbert, *The Modernist Garden in France*, New Haven, 1993; C. Garraud, *L'ideé de nature dans l'art contemporain*, Paris, 1994; U. Weilacher, *Between Landscape Architecture and Land*, Basel, 1996; G. Cooper, G. Taylor, *Paradise Transformed. The Private Garden for the Twenty-First Century*, New York, 1996; *Kathryn Gustafson: Sculpting the Land*, edited by L. Levy, Washington, 1998; M. Hucliez, *Jardins et parcs contemporains*, Paris, 1999; G. Donin, *Parchi/Parks*, Cannitello (Villa San Giovanni, Italy), 1999; *Architectural Record, Architectural Review, Blueprint, Gardens Illustrated, Jardin Passion, Landscape Design, Le Moniteur Architecture, Lotus navigator, Pages Paysages, SD Space Design, Topos.*

Esso Headquarters,
Rueil-Malmaison, 1992.

Jardins de l'Imaginaire,
Terrasson, 1996.

H

Richard Haag

Usa

1923

Bloedel Reserve,
Brainbridge Island,
Washington, 1978–85.

Richard Haag is one of the most important and influential landscape architects in America today. His two projects for Seattle, the Bloedel Reserve and the Gas Works Park, are among the most celebrated landscape works in the United States. In these designs Haag displays the countless opportunities that spring from minimal essential interventions in creating parks, introducing for the first time the theme of the recovery of abandoned industrial areas. Instead, in the small Jordan Park of Everett he uses debris from demolition fashioned in geometric shapes, covered with grass and connected by circuits, that become essential factors in a new environment. His approach to landscape reflects a number of different perspectives, including open references to the zen tradition, illustrated by Isamu Noguchi's work, as well as the simplicity of his own rural roots. The author of over five hundred designs, produced mainly in the American northwest, he is presently professor of Landscape Architecture at the University of Washington.

Gas Works Park, Seattle,
Washington, 1975.

Jordan Park, Everett,
Washington, 1970.

Works (a selection) Les Gove Park, Auburn, Washington, 1964; Jordan Park, Everett, Washington, 1970; Gas Works Park, Seattle, Washington, 1971–88; Bloedel Reserve, Brainbridge Island, Washington, 1978–85; Victor Steinbrueck Park, Seattle, Washington, 1984. **Selected bibliography** G. Cooper, G. Taylor, *Paradise Transformed. The Private Garden for the Twenty-First Century*, New York, 1996; *Richard Haag: Bloedel Reserve and Gas Works Park*, edited by W. S. Saunders, New York, 1998; *100 Years of Landscape Architecture: Some Patterns of a Century*, edited by M. Simo, Washington, 1999; *Abitare, Byggekunst, Garten und Landschaft, GSD News, Landscape Architecture, Landscape Australia, L'Architecture d'aujourd'hui, Places, Progressive Architecture, Quaderns d'arquitectura i urbanisme, Ville e Giardini*.

LAWRENCE HALPRIN

Lawrence
Halprin

Usa
1916

A landscape designer. After studying at the Universities of Cornell and Harvard, and training with Thomas Church, in 1949 he opened his own studio in San Francisco. His theory is based on the RSVP cycle (Resources, Score, Valuation, Performance), that elaborates designs aiming at creating landscapes that are always functional, emanating from actual needs and desires and, above all, accessible to everyone. The long list of his works thoroughly documents his over sixty years-long career: among his most famous works we should mention the Levi Strauss Park and Plaza in San Francisco, Sea Ranch on the Sonoma coast in California, the Lovejoy at Portland, the motorway park in Seattle and the more recent Franklin Delano Roosevelt Memorial and the Haas Promenade in Jerusalem. Obviously Halprin has worked on every scale of landscape, from a fountain to urban design and even a regional scale.

34

Portland Center,
Portland, Oregon, 1965.

*Franklin Delano
Roosevelt Memorial*,
Washington, 1997.

Works (a selection) Fairmount Hotel Roof Garden, San Francisco, California; Halprin Garden Kent Woodland, California, 1952–54; Lovejoy Plaza, Portland, Oregon, 1965–66; Anacostia River, master plan, Washington, 1968; Yerba Buena Gardens, master plan, San Francisco, California, 1969; Newport Beach Park, California, 1969–72; Portland Open Space Sequence, Portland, Oregon; Seattle Freeway Park, Seattle, Washington; Bunker Hill Steps, Los Angeles, California; Levi Strauss Park and Plaza, Corporate Headquarters, San Francisco, California; Haas Promenade, Jerusalem; Franklin Delano Roosevelt Memorial, Washington, 1997. **Selected bibliography** *Process Architecture 4: Lawrence Halprin*, February 1978; M. Emmanuel, *Contemporary Architects*, New York, 1980; L. Fortin, F. Oehmichen, R. Williams, *Histoire de l'architecture de paysage en Amérique du Nord*, Montréal, 1987; J. F. Frankel, *Modern Landscape Architecture: Defining the Garden*, New York, 1991; *The FDR Memorial: Designed by Lawrence Halprin*, Washington, 1998; M. Leccese, *American Eden. Landscape Architecture of the Pacific West*, Paris, 2000.

**George
Hargreaves**

Usa
1952

*Central Open Space
for the Olympics 2000,*
Sydney, 1996–2000.

Louisville Waterfront,
Louisville, Kentucky,
1990–99.

A landscape architect. In 1983 he founded the Hargreaves Associates studio with the purpose of making the landscape architecture discipline a part of the larger contemporary debate, striving to associate in his works both the city plan and architecture—without yielding to the traditional limitations of architecture and town planning—as well as art and science in the broadest sense. Natural processes outlining the orography of the site, materialized in patterns owed especially to the action of water and winds, become typical features in his designs. So the landscape created by Hargreaves is shaped and written anew, like a text, thanks to systems of signification and representation that are often immediately legible. Since 1991 he has been professor of the Practice of Landscape Architecture at Harvard University of Cambridge, Mass., as well as head of the department.

Works City Hall Plaza, Boston; Candlestick Point Cultural Park, San Francisco Bay; Byxbee Park, Palo Alto, California; Guadalupe River Park and Plaza Park, San José, California; Marugame Station Plaza, Marugame; Eastbank Riverfront Park, Portland, Oregon; Parque Tezozomoc, Mexico City; Todos Santos Plaza, Concord, California; Memorial Union North Courtyard, University of California, Davis, California; Arts Park, Los Angeles; Christie Avenue Plaza, Emeryville, California; Sigma Amphitheater, Library Square, Aronoff Center for Design, Art Architecture and Planning, University Commons, University of Cincinnati, Ohio; Fiddler's Green Amphitheater, Englewood, Colorado, 1984; Villa Zapu, Napa, California, 1986; Waterfront master plan, Louisville, Kentucky, 1992–99; Central Open Space for the Olympics 2000, Sydney, 1996–2000; Crissy Fiels Waterfront, San Francisco, 1996–2001; Dayton Residence and Garden, Minneapolis, Minnesota, 1997; Parque do Tejo e Trancão, Lisbon, 1998. **Selected bibliography** G. Hargreaves, "In Pursuit of the Real", in *Six Views: Contemporary Landscape Architecture,* edited by D. Frankel, Fullerton, 1986; S. A. Nash, *Facing Eden: 100 Years of Landscape Art in the Bay Area,* Berkeley, 1995; G. Cooper, G. Taylor, *Paradise Transformed: The Private Garden for the Twenty-First Century,* New York, 1996; *Redesigning City Squares and Plazas,* New York, 1997; M. Potteiger, J. Purinton, *Landscape Narratives,* New York, 1998; J. Beardsley, *Earthworks and Beyond,* New York, 1998; G. Taylor, *Gardens for the Future,* New York, 2000; I. Cortesi, *Il parco pubblico. Paesaggi 1985–2000,* Milan, 2000; M. Leccese, *American Eden. Landscape Architecture of the Pacific West,* Paris, 2000.

Louisville Waterfront,
Louisville, Kentucky,
1990–99.

Byxbee Park,
Palo Alto, California.

*Central Open Space
for the Olympics 2000*,
Sydney, 1996–2000.

"The object of the design should be the truth that the study of the environmental features brings to light"

HIROKI HASEGAWA, TORU MITANI

Japan

1958 and 1960

Hiroki Hasegawa and Toru Mitani, in their approach, make a subtle play on the ambiguous nature of a "site": "We work on the site as if it were by itself, and yet it is also an arbitrary, disconnected segment of a world that presently cannot be taken apart". They describe their contribution as "transitory". It tends to unify a place by suggesting and concretely rewriting its traces. In fact the new form always has something to do with what is already there, *in situ*, only apparently altered—for instance at Nakatsu the archaeological finds of several tombs that become a part of the final design. So it would seem the final outcome goes way beyond the mere elements or the designed space, if we wish to consider, as Toru Mitani suggests, that even a stone forming a hump on the landscape or a footprint can be a "site". The executed projects concern either city planning and design, or landscape architecture, or public area design.

36

*Ykk Research
and Development Center*,
Ryogoku, Tokyo, 1992–93.

Cozmix Building,
Niigata–shi, 1993–99.

Works Landscape for Natori Cultural Hall, Natori-shi, Miyagi, Japan, 1990–93; Ykk Research and Development Center Roof Garden, Ryogoku, Tokyo, 1992–93; Yokohama Portside Park, Yokohama, Japan, 1992–99; Landscape for Novartis Pharma, Tsukuba, Ibaraki, Japan, 1993; Park of Kaze-no-Oka Crematorium, Nkatsu, Oita, Japan, 1993–97 (with Fumihiko Maki); Osawano Kenko Fureai Park, Osawano cho. Toyama, Japan, 1993–99; Cozmix Building Installation, Niigata-shi, Japan, 1993–99; Isar Buro Park, Halbergmoos, Germany, 1994; Landscape for Town Center Building, Harima Science Park City, Hyogo, Japan, 1998; Courtyard of Setonaikai Broadcast Station, Takamatsu, Kagawa, Japan. **Selected bibliography** *A Pilgrimage in the Landscape*, Tokyo, 1990; J. Beardsley, *Earthworks and Beyond*, Tokyo, 1992; *A New Generation of Landscape Architects*, 1999; *Japan Landscape, LD, Lotus navigator, Nikkei Architecture, SD*.

Natori Cultural Hall,
Natori-shi, Miyagi, 1990–93.

Kaze-no-Oka Park,
Nakatsu, 1993–97.

Harima Science Park City,
Hyogo, 1998.

Osawano Kenko
Fureai Park, Osawano cho.
Toyama, 1993–99.

"We work on the site as if it existed on its own,   howeve

of a seamless world which   actuall

is also true that it is an arbitrary segment

mpossible to cut out in pieces"

MICHAEL HEIZER

Michael Heizer

Usa

1944

In 1966 Michael Heizer went back to roaming through the American deserts that his anthropologist father had shown him when he was a child. *North, East, South, West* (1967), *Nine Nevada Depressions* (1968) and *Primitive Dye Paintings* (1969) are some of the first works he did using local elements in the deserts of California and Nevada, that would become the stage and ideal setting for most of his works. A representative of the Land Art movement, with Walter De Maria and Robert Smithson, Heizer "works" with the outdoors, experimenting and creating large-scale interventions directly on the territory, seeking the place's primary, pre-historical state. In the great deserts, Heizer creates new finds; he designs archaeology with features recalling a culture that was there once or as a trace of a previous intelligence: the deep slashes in the Sierra Nevada contrast the rises and the verticality of the rock walls, deranging the setting they are placed in. A series of later works, *Effigy Tumuli* (1983–85), shows how in his interventions his interest in geometry evolved toward semi-abstract forms.

 # 8 of Nine Nevada Depressions, Black Rock Desert, Nevada, 1968.

Double Negative, Mormon Mesa, Overton, Nevada, 1969–70.

#1 of Nine Nevada Depressions, Massacre Dry Lake, Nevada, 1968.

Works (a selection) North, East, South, West, 1967; Isolated Mass, Circumflex, Nine Nevada Depressions, Massacre Dry Lake, Nevada, 1968; Rift, Nine Nevada Depressions, Massacre Dry Lake, Nevada, 1968; Dissipate, Nine Nevada Depressions, Massacre Dry Lake, Nevada, 1968; Primitive Dye Paintings, 1969; Double Negative, Mormon Mesa, Overton, Nevada, 1969–70; Complex One (1972–74), Complex Two (1980–88), Complex Three (1980–99), Garden Valley, Nevada; Rift 2, 1982; Water Strider, Buffalo Rock, 1983–85; City, 2000. **Exhibitions** Heizer's work was presented in "When Attitudes Become Forms", Bern Kunsthalle (1969), and at Documenta VI (1977). His one-man shows include the ones at the Heiner Friedrich Galerie in Munich (1969) and at the Museum of Contemporary Art of Los Angeles (1984). **Selected bibliography** M. Heizer, *Dragged Mass Geometric*, New York, 1984; J. Brown, B. Heizer, *Michael Heizer: Sculpture in Reverse*, Los Angeles, 1984; D. G. McGill, *Effigy Tumuli. The Reemergence of Ancient Mound Building*, New York, 1990; D. Whitney, *Michael Heizer*, London, 1990; M. C. Taylor, *Michael Heizer: Double Negative*, Los Angeles-New York, 1992; G. Celant, *Michael Heizer*, Milan, 1996; *Land and Environmental Art*, edited by J. Kastner and B. Willis, Hong Kong, 1998.

NANCY HOLT

Nancy Holt

Usa
1938

She lived and worked in New York from 1960 to 1995, then moved to Galisteo in New Mexico. Nancy Holt creates films, videotapes, installations, gardens, as well as sculptures for public areas; her sculptures essentially have to do with perception, space and ecology, and are connected with the topography, the psychology and the history of each place. Using concrete, prefabricated construction elements—bricks, stone walls, earth and steel— Holt makes structures that surround and enclose the public, while creating, by building openings and tunnels, the impression that the space is expanding. Her sculptures relate symbolically to the courses of the sunlight and moonlight, to astronomical alignments and reflections on water. Her many works for public areas, including the *Sun Tunnels* (1973–76) in the Utah desert, *Catch Basin* (1982) at Toronto, and *Sole Source* (1983) in Dublin, are some of the highlights of the Land Art movement.

Sun Tunnels,
Great Basin Desert,
Utah, 1973–76.

Solar Rotary, Tampa,
Florida, 1995.

Works (a selection) Buried Poem, photographs, Arches National Park, Utah, 1971; Sun Tunnels, Great Basin Desert, Utah, 1973–76; Hydra's Head, Niagara Riverbank, Artpark, Lewiston, New York, 1974; Stone Enclosure: Rock Rings, Western University Grounds, Bellingham, Washington, 1977–78; Star-Crossed, Miami University Art Museum, Oxford, Ohio, 1979–81; Solar Rotary, Tampa, Florida, 1995. **Selected bibliography** *The Writings of Robert Smithson*, edited by N. Holt, New York, 1979; G. A. Tiberghien, *Land Art*, Paris, 1993; *Land and Environmental Art*, edited by J. Kastner and B. Willis, Hong Kong, 1998.

WALTER J. HOOD

Walter J. Hood

Usa
1951

Walter Hood's research is always directed toward interpreting and under-standing the characteristics of the American multiracial society, enquiring into the aspects most related to the urban landscape. His designing approach analyzes first of all the environmental features expressing the time, the social uses and the resources of a place. Written and oral family histories, activities and existing elements are then assembled in a process that is able to rebuild, in an "alternative" and "improvised" way, a new city landscape, recreating its most meaningful cultural, environmental features and physical complexities. At Oakland, at Macon and San Francisco the pursuit of visual continuity, the themes related to the connection and social use of the spaces give rise to typological hybrids, public areas where streets, plazas and facilities mingle with tree-lined walkways. His professional and theoretic activity is completed by teaching, as professor and chairman at the University of California at Berkeley.

Lafayette Square,
Oakland, California, 2000.

Courtland Creek Park,
Oakland, California, 1997.

Works Courtland Creek Park, Oakland, California, 1990–97; Lafayette Square, Oakland, California, 1995–99; Poplar Street Improvement Project, Macon, Georgia, 1998–2000; Yerba Buena Lane, San Francisco, California, 1998–2000 (with Cheryl Barton); Richmond Neighborhood Project, Richmond, California, 1999–2000; The National Underground Railroad Museum, Cincinnati, Ohio, 1999–2001 (with Martha Schwartz); The New De Young Museum, San Francisco, California, 2000 (with Herzog & De Meuron). **Selected bibliography** W. Hood, *Blues and Jazz Landscapes*, Berkeley, 1993; W. Hood, *CITY: Issues of African-American Urban Space*, Los Angeles, 1994; W. Hood, *Urban Diaries*, Washington, 1997; *"Everyday Urbanism"*, New York, 1999; W. Hood, *Design Culture Now: National Design Triennial, Cooper Hewitt, National Design Museum, Smithsonian Institution*, New York, 2000.

Lafayette Square,
Oakland, California, 2000.

Courtland Creek Park,
Oakland, California, 1997.

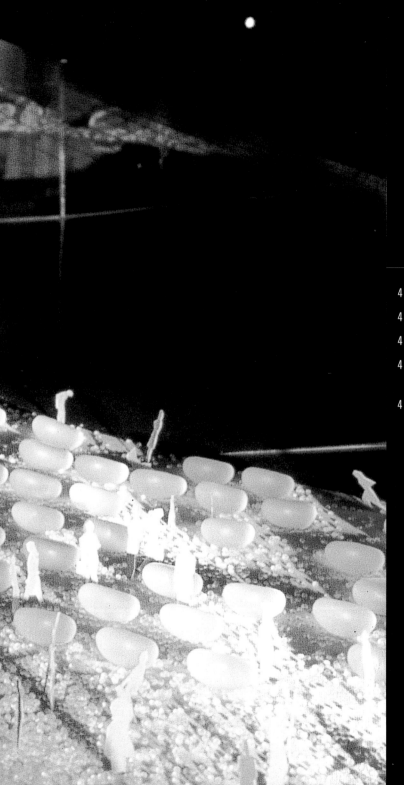

I J

Robert Irwin

Usa
1928

His latest design for the Getty Foundation gardens in Los Angeles should not lead us to overlook the major contribution his works have brought to American art in the past decades, nor the variety of fields he dealt in and that led to this "trespassing". In the seventies, while Minimal Art was glorifying the material and the object, Californian artists, including Irwin, created dematerialized environments, silent and empty spaces, turned within, indicated only by minimal changes in the architecture or by a particular arrangement of the light sources. In the eighties and the nineties, Irwin traded the empty, immaculate museum space for the concrete space of an urban site, but the radical nature of his intervention did not change. What interests him is not the object or the sculpture but the space around it, not the solid but the void, where the experience of vision occurs. In striving to explore the illusory and dynamic nature of perception the artist borrows some of his language from phenomenonology. He appeals to the viewers' active perception and reflection believed essential for creating individual values (and therefore, indirectly, as a social action).

ROBERT IRWIN

40

Lowel Central Garden,
The Getty Center,
Los Angeles,
California, 1997.

One-man shows Pace Gallery, New York, 1966; Pace Gallery, New York, 1968; MoMA, New York, 1970–71; San Francisco Museum of Art, San Francisco, California, 1973; Whitney Museum of American Art, New York, 1977; University of California Art Museum, Berkeley, California, 1979; Pace Gallery, New York, 1992; Lowel Central Garden, The Getty Center, Los Angeles, California, 1997; Museum of Contemporary Art, San Diego, California, 1997; Dia Center for the Arts, New York, 1998; Pace Gallery, New York, 1998. **Selected bibliography** *Robert Irwin*, New York, 1977; L. Wechsler, *Seeing Is Forgetting the Name of the Thing One Sees: A Life of Contemporary Artist Robert Irwin*, Berkeley, 1982; R. Irwin, *Being and Circumstance: Notes Towards a Conditional Art*, Larkspur Landing, California, 1985; *Robert Irwin*, Los Angeles, 1993; G. Cooper, G. Taylor, *Gardens for the Future*, New York, 2000.

"A sculpture shaped like a garden
that aspires to be art"

MOTOKO ISHII

Motoko Ishii

Japan

The installations by Motoko Ishii, like the ones by Tahara Keiichi and Walter De Maria, belong to a technological naturalism that strives to recreate a primeval, natural, non-humanized world. This approach entails a sophisticated relationship with technology and the environment, since it begins with the assumption of a situation previously altered by the proliferation of artificial images. And yet places become virtual images as soon as they are chosen to be the theatre of the action, and the intervention merely consists in selecting a few elements of the landscape, or excluding or drawing attention to a specific aspect. At Okinawa for instance, Ishii created a system of underwater lighting along about a kilometre of coral reef. Sixty lamps, at varying depths, illuminate the ocean, creating an undefined form entirely free of technological connotations: the natural factor of the coral reef is represented by a simulation, a virtualization of the context (like at Yokohama) in which a *natura artificialis* is recreated by an effect of fluorescence.

Grand Mall Park, Yokohama Minato Mirai, 1989.

Ocean Expo'75, Okinawa, 1975.

Works Ocean Expo '75, Okinawa, 1975; Grand Mall Park, Yokohama, 1989; Light up Hakodate, Hokkaido, 1990; Gifu Memorial Center, Gifu, 1991; Light up of Nara Park, Nara, 1992; Nagasaki Holland Village Huis Ten Bosch, Nagasaki, 1992; Light up Himeji, Hyogo, 1993; Rainbow Bridge, Tokyo, 1993; Fukuoka Dome Light-illusion, Fukuoka, 1994; Yebisu Garden Place, Tokyo, 1994; City Light Plan in Nagasaki, Nagasaki, 1994; Kema Sakuranomiya Park, Osaka, 1995; Miyazaki Tachibana Park, Miyazaki, 1995. **Selected bibliography** *Design for Environmental Lighting*, Tokyo, 1984; *My World of Light*, Tokyo, 1985; *Light to Infinity*, Tokyo, 1991; *Journey to my Heartland-Finland*, Japan Broadcast, 1996; *Creation of Lightscape by Motoko Ishii*, Tokyo, 1997.

TOYO ITO

Toyo Ito

Corea
1941

Tokyo Frontier Project.

O Dome, Odate,
Akita, 1997.

Sendai Mediatheque,
Miyagi, 1999–2001.

He worked from 1965 to 1969 in the studio of Kiyonori Kikutake, one of the leading figures of the Metabolism trend, and opened his own studio in 1971. Ito uses organic expressions, in part focused on the transformations of nature, climate and wind, associated with the theme of transparency and the study of outdoor spaces. Works like the Tower of Winds (Yokohama, 1986) and Egg of Winds (Tokyo, 1991), and the more recent Sendai Mediatheque (2001) or the Health Pavilion in Hanover represent an amazingly creative and original proof of the opportunities offered by new technologies. Ito's research answers the need to find a proper space for the ideal life in an era saturated with information: architectural gestures that "should invent the screen that makes it possible to visualize the air laden with information and not yet visualized". He is honorary professor of the University of North London.

TOYO ITO

42

Works (a selection) White U, Tokyo, 1976; Silver Hut, Tokyo, 1984; Tower of Winds, Yokohama, 1986; Restaurant Nomad, Tokyo, 1986; Guest-house of the Sapporo Brewery, Hokkaido, 1989; Building T, Nakameguro, Tokyo, 1990; Town Hall, Yatsushiro, Kumamoto, 1991; Egg of Winds, Tokyo, 1991; Hotel P, Shari-Gun, Hokkaido, 1992; Town Museum, Shimosuwa, 1993; ITM Building, Matsuyama, Ehime, 1993; Amusement Park H, Tokyo, 1993; Town Kindergarten Eckenheim, Frankfurt am Main, 1993; Old People's Home, Yatsushiro, Kumamoto, 1994; Fire Brigade Barracks, Yatsushiro, Kumamoto, 1995; Theatre and Concert Hall, Nagaoka, Niigata, 1996; Hotel Complex, Otaku, Nigata, 1997; O Dome, Odate, Akita, 1997; Town Hall, Notsuharu, Oita, 1998; Sendai Mediatheque, Miyagi, 1999–2001; Health Pavilion, Expo 2000, Hanover, 2000. **Monographs** S. Roulet. S. Soulie, *Toyo Ito*, Paris, 1991; *Toyo Ito*, Barcelona, 1997; *Toyo Ito*, edited by A. Maffei, Milan, 2001.

Charles Jencks
& Maggie Keswick

Great Britain
1939
1945-1995

Charles Jencks, more known for his critical essays on post-modern architecture, and his wife Maggie Keswick, an expert in Chinese gardens, created the Cosmological Garden in the south-west of Scotland, at Dumfriesshire. Occupying a surface of about 16 hectares, the park appears to be a spectacular metaphor of the theory of chaos and complexity, of Benoît Mandelbrot's fractal geometry, while being deeply inspired by the Chinese feng shui lesson on energy curves. The design of curves, waves, terraces, expanses of water and circuits, for the most part produced by earthwork, only covered by grass and scattered with rare extraneous elements, responds to the attempt to combine the traditional art of gardening with these two scientific theories. The garden looks like a new Earth Art operation, where the sculptures modelled in earth and grass design in three dimensions the lines of energy flowing through the universe.

Cosmological Garden,
Dumfriesshire, Scotland,
1990.

Works Cosmological Garden, Dumfriesshire, Scotland, 1990; Dna and Physics Garden, The Border, Scotland, 2000. **Selected bibliography** M. Keswick, *The Chinese Garden: History, Art & Architecture, London-New York,* 1986; C. Jencks, "New Science - New Architecture", in *A+U,* June 1995; G. Cooper, G. Taylor, *Paradise Transformed. The Private Garden for the Twenty-First Century,* New York, 1996; G. Cooper, G. Taylor, *Gardens for the Future,* New York, 2000.

JENSEN & SKODVIN

Jan Olav Jensen
& Børre Skodvin

Norway
1959 and 1960

Mountain Roads,
Norway, 1995–98.

Especially known for their recent prize-winning project in the competition for the rest areas set out along the Norwegian tourist circuits, Jensen and Skodvin have succeeded in using minimal interventions to "order the landscape", introducing features that seek to reveal the geometries in nature. The project comprises several interventions that include developing new elements to place along the circuit (signs, bulwarks, furniture) and creating new rest areas. Parking lots, signs and information points, equipped circuits, instead of being colonizing features in the natural landscape, become authentic, distinguished architectural designs. The project entails localized interventions, determined by the geometric perspective from the individual site and therefore unique, as well as designs of generic articles that can be used in various places and whose shape depends on their function.

Projects Mountain Roads, Norway, 1995–98; Roof for Parking, Oslo Airport, 1997–98; House Wormdal, Haug, Oslo, 1989–91; Mortensrud Church, Oslo, 1999–2000. **Selected bibliography** *Architectural Review, Area, Arkitethi, A+U, Baumeister, Byggenkunst, Domus, L'Architecture d'aujourd'hui, Lotus international, Spazio e Società, 9H.*

ANISH KAPOOR

Anish Kapoor

India
1954

Born in Bombay, he has lived and worked in Great Britain since the early seventies. Anish Kapoor is an artist who uses stone, marble, pigment, stainless steel and plaster. Drawing on elementary materials, including water and air, his research focuses on concepts of material and immaterial, on the idea of gravity and lightness, of surface and space, sight and sound, achieving a subtle balance between reality and illusion by appealing to all the senses. Lately Kapoor's works have explored the concept of "void": the artist deeply incises the stone, occasionally applies colour to the inside and the void becomes a vibrant, shadowy space. In other works, such as the ones for the Hayward Gallery, he investigates the transformation of space: the work penetrates the walls and the paving, giving the impression it is being produced by the architecture. In his sculptures his fascination for the dark and for light is just apparent; the interactions between form and light produced by the translucid quality of the resin, the pigment, the alabaster and the flowing reflections of stainless steel and water seek to suggest fundamental physical and psychological experiences and conditions.

1000 Names, 1982.

Building for a Void, 1992.

*Black Stones,
Human Bones*, 1993.

45

ANISH KAPOOR

Exhibitions Kunsthalle, Basel, 1985; Biennale di Venezia, Venice, 1990; Museum of Contemporary Art, San Diego, California, 1992; Galerie Thaddaeus Ropac, Paris, 1993; Barbara Gladstone, New York, 1993; Stuart Regen Gallery, Los Angeles, California, 1994; Fondazione Prada, Milan, 1995; CAPC Bordeaux, Bordeaux, France, 1998; Lisson Gallery, London, 1998; Barbara Gladstone, New York, 1998. **Selected bibliography** *Anish Kapoor. Beeldhouwwerken*, Rotterdam, 1983; *Feeling into Form*, Liverpool, 1983; *Anish Kapoor*, Basel, 1985; *Anish Kapoor: Works on Paper 1975–1987*, Sydney, 1987; *Blau: Farbe der Ferne*, edited by H. Gerke, Heidelberg, 1990; *Anish Kapoor*, Madrid, 1992; *Anish Kapoor*, Tel Aviv, 1993; *Anish Kapoor*, Ljubljana, 1994; G. Celant, *Anish Kapoor*, Milan, 1995.

DANI KARAVAN

Dani Karavan

Israel

1930

Trained in Tel Aviv and Florence, through his art Dani Karavan strives to find in nature a universal harmony that is often missing in reality. He is constantly engaged in creating places of remembrance, and his installations give sculpture a public role: to conserve the memory of the past. They are created as sensory circuits, specific itineraries, visions that require the visitor's participation. The recurrent themes of peace and tolerance are expressed by symbolic forms, elementary and minimal, coarse materials chosen to adjust to the climate and the site, or else by reversed natural elements excluding any possible harmony. After his monument in the Negev, in which every means of expression aims at total integration with the site, and his work at the 1976 Venice Biennale, that won him his first international acclaim, and up to the imperial Award for sculpture in 1998, Karavan's installations have been conceived as a great metaphor, rather like immediately accessible communication devices.

DANI KARAVAN

46

Passages, Homage to Walter Benjamin, Port-Bou, 1990–94.

Denmark Junior High School, Jerusalem, 1969–70.

Works (a selection) Court of Justice, Tel Aviv, 1960–64; Negev Monument, Beersheba, Israel, 1963–68; Environment in stone, metal sphere and olive trees, Denmark Junior High School, Jerusalem, 1969–70; Environment for Peace, 38th Biennale di Venezia, Venice, 1976; Kikara Levana, Tel Aviv, 1977–88; Two Environments for Peace, Forte Belvedere, Florence, 1978; Two Environments for Peace, Castello dell'Imperatore, Prato, Italy, 1978; Documenta VI, Kassel; Ma'alot, Museum Ludwig, Cologne, Germany, 1979–86; Axe Majeur, Cergy-Pontoise, France, 1980; Linea 1.2.3. + 4, Fattoria di Celle, Pistoia, Italy, 1980–85; The Way to the Philosopher Path, Kunstverein, Hildemberg, Germany, 1983; Way of Light, Olympic Sculpture Park, Seoul, 1987–88; Dialogue, Wilhelm-Lehmbruck Museum, Duisburg, Germany, 1989; Ohel, Shina Hospital, Tel Hashomer, Israel, 1990–91; Passages, Homage to Walter Benjamin, Port-Bou, Spain, 1990–94; Garden of the Pioneers, Hedera, Israel, 1991–99; Homage to the Ancient Prisoners of Camp, Gurs, France, 1993–94; Village Plaza, Crédit Suisse, Horgen, Switzerland, 1994–95; Place de la Tolérance, Unesco, Paris, 1996; Intifada, Ramatgan, Israel, 1997; Garden of Memories, Duisburg, Germany, 1999; Nursery for Peace, Pistoia, Italy, 1999; Way to the Hidden Garden, Sapporo, Japan, 1999–2000. **Monographs** *Dani Karavan*, edited by P. Restany, Munich, 1992.

Way to the Hidden Garden,
Sapporo, 1999–2000.

Linea 1. 2. 3. + 4,
Fattoria di Celle,
Pistoia, 1980–85.

Axe Majeur,
Cergy-Pontoise, 1980.

DIETER KIENAST

Dieter Kienast

Switzerland
1945-1998

After training as a gardener, he settled in Germany where he graduated from the University of Kassel, then beginning a long landscaping career in Switzerland. Nature and culture live together in gardens, parks and plazas, which for Kienast play an important mediatorial role: in these spaces we can learn once again how to face nature, less to master it than to use it actively. A few years ago in an article for the review *Lotus international* he outlined a decalogue of his design theories: the advantage of variety over uniformity, of diversity over homologation, heterogeneity opposed to monoculture; the quest for an "urban nature" to which trees, hedges and lawns belong, but roads, plazas, artificial elements and non-natural colours as well, and a particular attention to urban non-places; the notion that the design is an expression of the culture of the times and respect for the site. His works are outstanding by the clear distinction they draw between the concepts of "nature" and "garden", by their rigorous, sophisticated geometric composition, avoiding naturalistic references, and that he associates with simple elements, plant essences and sculptural and architectural presences.

Nature n'existe pas,
Chaumont-sur-Loire, 1996.

Et in Arcadia ego,
Uetliberg, 1989–94.

In Praise of Ambiguity,
Bavaria, 1995.

Mimesis, Greifensee, 1995.

Works (a selection) Et in Arcadia ego, Uetliberg, Switzerland, 1989–94; Gartenanlagen der Psychiatrischen Klinik Waldhaus, Chur, Switzerland, 1990–96; Umgebungsgestaltung Wohnüberbauung Vogelbach, Riehen, Switzerland, 1991–92; Die Garten der Klinik Hirslanden, Zurich, 1991–97; Verwaltungsgebäude Swisscom, Worblaufen, Bern, 1993–98; Umgebungsgestaltung Geschäftshaus Suva, Basel, 1994; Umgebungsgestaltung Hotel Zürichberg, Zurich, 1994; Neubau Madagaskarhalle, Zurich Zoo, 1994; Umgebungsgestaltung Ricola, Brunnstatt, France, 1994; Siedlung Neustädter Feld, Magdeburg, Switzerland, 1994; Neugestaltung Augustusplatz, Leipzig, 1994; Wohnüberbauung Silhof und Verwaltungsgebäude, Adliswil im Silhof, Switzerland, 1994–95; Platz und Garten zum Regierungsgebäude, Chur, Switzerland, 1994–95; Mimesis, Greifensee, Switzerland, 1995; Geschäftshaus Ernst Basler & Partner, Zurich, 1995–96; Die Freiflächen des Zentrums für Kunst, Karlsruhe, 1995–97; Nature n'existe pas, Chaumont-sur-Loire, France, 1996; Umgebungsgestaltung Swiss Re, Paris, 1996–97; Stadtgarten am Neubau des Bundesarbeitsgerichts, Erfurt, 1996–99; Innenhofgestaltung Geschätshaus der Swiss Re, Zurich, 1997; Umgebungsgestaltung Spar-und Landeskasse, Fürstenfeldbruck, 1997; Seminar- und Ausbildungszentrum det Swiss Re, Rüschlikon, 1997–2000; Umgebungsgestaltung Ricola, Laufen, 1998; Umgebungsgestaltung Museum Liner, Appenzell, 1998. **Selected bibliography** U. Weilacher, *Between Landscape Architecture and Land Art*, Berlin-Basel-Boston, 1996; D. Kienast, *Garten=gardens. Dieter Kienast*, Basel, 1997; D. Kienast, *Kienast Vogt. Aussenräume open spaces*, Berlin, 1999; I. Cortesi, *Il parco pubblico. Paesaggi 1985–2000*, Milan, 2000. For a number of years he was editor of the review *Anthos*; his works are published in *Anthos, Archithese, Aktuelles Bauen, Arquitectura Viva, Bauwelt, Lotus international, Lotus navigator, Mitteilungen der Gesellschaft für Gartenkultur, Topos*.

"Our task is to seek 'urban nature', whose colour
is not just green, but grey, too: trees, hedges,
lawns belong to it, but roads, plazas,
artificial canals, walls, penetration and ventilation
axes, centre and outskirts as well"

DAN URBAN KILEY

Dan
Urban Kiley

Usa
1912

Considered the "dean of landscape architects in the United States", ever since his first works in the fifties he has stood for a break with the traditional models of European gardens, urging greater care for the particular topographical and natural conditions of the various regional American landscapes. Kiley himself expressed his approach to landscape design a number of times, using the simile of a walk amidst nature, where everything is real, and where this dynamic experience alters the settings' features, even though they remain "appropriate" to the context. The acknowledgment of the wealth of the American landscape, inspired by his rapport with the first landscape painters and Frederick Law Olmsted's designs, and the use of geometric models for garden design, recalling André Le Nôtre's gardens, are two possible principles for interpreting Kiley's lengthy career, which includes the Jefferson National Expansion Memorial at St. Louis, in collaboration with Eero Saarinen, and the water garden featuring the four hundred fountains of Fountain Place in front of the Dallas City Bank designed by Pei and Cobb.

DAN URBAN KILEY

48

*Henry Moore
Sculpture Garden,*
Nelson Atkins Museum,
Kansas City, 1989.

Ford Foundation,
New York, 1964
(with K. Roche
and J. Dinkeloo).

Works (a selection) St. Louis Arch Park, St. Louis, 1947; Irwin Miller Garden, Columbus, Indiana, 1955; Dulles International Airport, Chantilley, Virginia, 1958; Currier Farm, Dandby, Vermont, 1959; Art Institute of Chicago South Garden, Chicago, 1962; Hamilton Residence, Columbus, Ohio, 1963; Ford Foundation, New York, 1964 (with K. Roche and J. Dinkeloo); Oakland Museum, Oakland, California, 1969; John F. Kennedy Library, Boston, Massachusetts, 1978; Water Sculpture, La Défense, Paris, 1978; Dallas Art Museum, Dallas, Texas, 1985; Fountain Place, Dallas, Texas, 1985–87; Nelson Atkins Museum, Henry Moore Sculpture Garden, Kansas City, Missouri, 1987–89; Garden, Brentwood, California, 1992; Corning Riverfront Centennial Park, New York, 1992; Lehr Residence Garden, Miami Beach, Florida, 1993. **Selected bibliography** *The Work of Dan Kiley. A Dialogue on Design Theory,* edited by W. T. Byrd and M. Rainey, Charlottesville, 1983; *The American Landscape, Christian Zapatka,* edited by M. Zardini, New York, 1996; G. Cooper, G. Taylor, *Paradise Transformed. The Private Garden for the Twenty-First Century,* New York, 1996; D. Kiley, J. Amidon, *Dan Kiley: The Complete Works of America's Master Landscape Architect,* London-Boston, 1998; W. S. Saunders, *Daniel Urban Kiley,* New York, 1999; G. R. Hildebrand, *The Miller Garden: Icon of Modernism,* Washington, 1999; *Dan Urban Kiley: The Early Gardens,* New York, 2000.

Fountain Place,
Dallas, 1987.

REM KOOLHAAS - OMA

Rem Koolhaas
Oma

Netherlands
1944

Museumpark,
Rotterdam, 1992–94.

In 1974, with Madelon Vriesendorp, Elia and Zoe Zenghelis, he founded the Office for Metropolitan Architecture (Oma). Since the competition for the Parc de La Villette in Paris in 1983 and the next one for the "Ville Nouvelle" of Melun-Sénart, Oma's designs have propounded a horizontal development of the territory: they deal with the landscape in its extension rather than the usual "vertical" concentration of buildings. The new outlines of the landscape, thus traced, can absorb, especially in connection with the facilities, a variety of urban programmes and situations surrounding scattered constructions. At Lille, in an area within the bounds of the city, but also excluded by avenues, expressways and railways, Koolhaas created an urban development that tends to "exacerbate complexity, taking it to a magic point where problems become potentials".

Works (a selection) Competition for the Parc de La Villette, Paris, 1983 (with B. Tschumi); Nexus Residential Ensemble at Fukuoka, Japan, 1991; Museumpark, Rotterdam, 1992–94; Euralille, Lille, France, 1994–; Landscape design, Chin Suei Service Area, Taiwan (with M. Botta, J. Nouvel, T. Farnell), 1996; Landscape design, H-Project, Seoul, Korea, 1996; Public Park design, Niederlandische Botschaft, Berlin, 2000. **Selected bibliography** *Oma, Rem Koolhaas: pour une culture de la congestion*, edited by J. Lucan, Paris, 1990; R. Koolhaas, *S, M, L, XL*, New York, 1995; R. Koolhaas, *Delirious New York: A Retroactive Manifesto for Manhattan*, New York, 1995; R. Koolhaas, *Oma 30: 30 colours / Rem Koolhaas*, Boston, 1998; J. Lucan, R. Koolhaas, *Oma, Rem Koolhaas Living, Vivre, Leben*, Birkhauser, 1999; R. Koolhaas, B. Colenbrander, M. Provoost, *Dutchtown: A City Center Design by Oma/Rem Koolhaas*, Nai Publishers, 2000.

KENGO KUMA

Kengo Kuma

Japan
1954

"We should not just view architecture and landscape design as two inseparable parts of a same action, but we should recover the gardener's techniques and apply them to architecture." With these basic assumptions, Kengo Kuma's designs prevailingly deal with transforming the landscape, offering solutions that blend the Japanese garden tradition with the very latest trends in art and technology. Kuma's other idea is to turn the environment and the object into a continuum, introducing sounds, patterns and smells by using digital technology: the landscape appears set in an architectural frame that tends to become invisible, and is always conceived as an outlooking observatory. In the Memorial Park at Gumna, the garden features a more traditional part, defined by the design of the circuits, spaces and essences, and an immaterial part, where interactive software guides the visitor through the complex experience of the circuit. In the Ando Hiroshige Museum the architecture consists of a system of wooden fences that make the building become a light "sensor" and that change with the variations of the illumination.

Kitami Canal Museum, Kitakami, 1998.

Ando Hiroshige Museum, Tochigi, 2000.

Water/Glass House, Shizuoka, 1995.

Works Bathhouse, Izu, Shizuoka, Japan, 1988; Kyodo Grating, Tokyo, 1988; Gunma Toyota, Maebashi, Japan, 1989; Maiton Resort, Phuket, Thailand, 1991; Miyagi Zao Resort Condominium, Miyagi, Japan, 1992; Kinojo Golf Club, Okayama, Japan, 1992; Yusuhara Visitor's Center, Kochi, Japan, 1994; Kirosan Observatory, Ehime, Japan, 1994; Japanese Pavilion, Biennale di Venezia, Venice, 1995; Toyoma Center for Performing Arts, Toyoma, Japan; Water/Glass House, Shizuoka, Japan, 1995; Observatory, Oshima, Japan; Tomioka Lakewood Golf Club, Gunma, Japan, 1996; Noh Stage in Forest, Miyagi, Japan, 1996; Memorial Park, Gunma, Japan, 1996; Awasi Service Area, Hyogo, Japan, 1998; Kitami Canal Museum, Kitakami, Japan, 1998–; Ando Hiroshige Museum, Tochigi, Japan, 2000. **Selected bibliography** *Kisho Kurokawa, New Wave Japanese Architecture*, London, 1993; *Labyrinth: New Generation in Japanese Architecture*, Tokyo, 1993; K. Kuma, *An Introduction to Architectural History and Ideology*, Chikuma, 1994; K. Kuma, *The Catastrophe of Architectural Desire*, Shinyosha, 1994; K. Kuma, *Beyond the Architectural Crisis*, Tokyo, 1995; K. Kuma, *Kengo Kuma: Geometries of Nature*, Milan, 1999.

"I want to eliminate architecture. I have always wanted to

and I don't think I shall change my mind"

Kirosan Observatory,
Ehime, 1994.

Memorial Park,
Gunma, 1996.

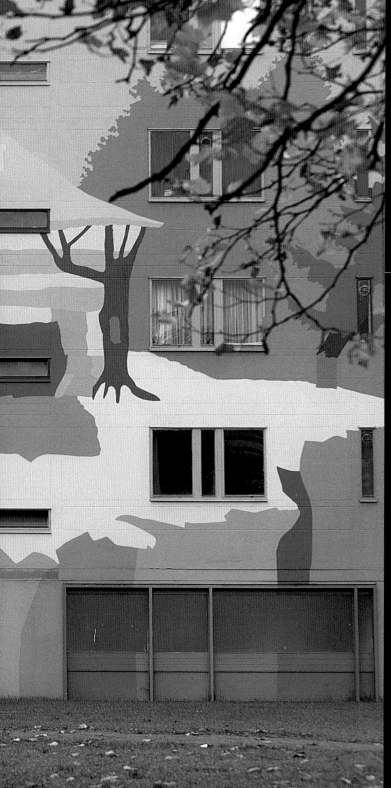

L

MARTINEZ LAPEÑA, TORRES TUR

José A. Martinez
Lapeña
Elias Torres Tur

Spain
1941 and 1944

Park of Castelldefels,
Barcelona, 1987–94.

Nizayama
Forest Art Museum,
Nizayama, 1998.

After training at the Escola Tècnica Superior d'Arquitectura in Barcelona, in 1968 they began to work together creating projects for public areas and buildings. The gardens by José Lapeña and Elias Torres appear to set up and arrange, according to their own rules, fragments of nature inside a limited, measurable city space. This is the case at Girona, where an enclosure separates and shields the garden from the roads and where the sense of playfulness and surreality is emphasized by countless elements and quotations of typically local features or ones drawn from the vernacular. On the other hand the layout of the garden of the Villa Cecilia in Barcelona seems to cull its references from the Baroque garden tradition—hedges and circuits forming curved, winding patterns, labyrinths—to transform them, reinventing multiple areas and hidden places. They are both professors at the ETSAB.

51

Works (a selection) Gardens of Villa Cecília, Barcelona, 1985–87; Park of Castelldefels, Barcelona, 1987–94; Plaza de la Constitución, Girona, Spain, 1990–92; Regina Sofía Park, Cadix, Spain, 1990–95; Restoration of the City Walls, Palma di Majorca, Spain; Nizayama Forest Art Museum, Japan, 1998; Kamitaira-Mura Reception Building and Gardens, Japan. **Selected bibliography** I. Cortesi, *Il parco pubblico. Paesaggi 1985–2000*, Milan, 2000; *Architectural Review, Casabella, Detail, El Croquis, L'Architecture d'aujourd'hui, Progressive Architecture, Space Design.*

Gardens of Villa Cecilia,
Barcelona, 1985–87.

Regina Sofía Park,
Cadix, 1990–95.

Restoration of the City Walls,
Palma de Majorca.

BERNARD LASSUS

Bernard Lassus

France

1929

Bernard Lassus is one of the most original and creative French landscape architects; his works, in a career of almost forty years, have always expressed the intent to develop and organize a code for grasping and reformulating the concept of landscape in its broadest sense. From his early works, influenced by contemporary artists, borrowing and using their light and pure colours, to the creation of small areas on the margins of the industrial city, always with the idea of "playing" the "garden game", his gardens have often been judged merely extravagant, whereas they appear strongly characterized by the presence of whimsical hints and daring design solutions. His creations always suggest a new interpretation of the work, turning the visitors into active spectators invited to re-examine their own perceptions of the world in an infinitely suggestive place like a garden. Presently he is engaged in a number of works related to the environmental revitalization of motorway segments (Angers-Tours; Tours-Vierzon; Alençon-Le Mans).

A85 Motorway,
Angers-Tours.

BERNARD LASSUS

52

A837 Rest Area of the
Pierre de Crazannes,
Crazannes, 1995.

Les Buissons Optiques,
Niort, 1993.

Works (a selection) Le serpent et les papillons, Passerelle d'Istres, France, 1981; Parc de la Corderie Royale, Rochefort-sur-Mer, France, 1988; Garden of the Château de Barbirey-sur-Ouche, France; Les Buissons Optiques, Niort, France, 1993; A837 Rest Area of the Pierre de Crazannes, Crazannes, France, 1995; Jardin des Retours, Rochefort-sur-Mer, France, 2000–. **Selected bibliography** B. Lassus, *Le Jardin de l'Antérieur*, 1975; B. Lassus, *Jardins imaginaires*, Paris, 1975; B. Lassus, *Jeux*, Paris, 1977; *Villes-Paysages, couleurs en Lorraine*, Paris, 1990; *Le Jardin des Tuileries de Bernard Lassus*, London, 1991; B. Lassus, *Une poétique du paysage: le démesurable*, Paris-Vancouver, 1991; *Hypothèses pour une troisième nature*, edited by B. Lassus, London, 1992; C. Leyrit, B. Lassus, *Autoroute et paysages*, Paris, 1994; B. Lassus, *The Landscape Approach*, Philadelphia, 1998; P. Poullaouec-Gonidec, M. Gariépy, B. Lassus, *Le Paysage territoire d'intention*, Montréal, 1999; I. Cortesi, *Il parco pubblico. Paesaggi 1985–2000*, Milan, 2000.

Peter Latz

Germany
1939

A town-planner and landscape architect, he has treated for many years the theme of the revitalization of blighted industrial areas, transforming the old productive centres by a progressive reinterpretation of these "complex places", which can comprise activities of production, housing, recreation, ecological renaturalization and the rediscovery of traces of history. Latz approaches redesigning the landscape with a praxis that by now is established, and in a sequence of phases that range from the renovation of the connection circuits, to the creation of new gardens and pavings—using waste—to the recovery of some items that recall their previous function. Although Latz' public parks retain some historicized elements, they offer an unusual view of the possibilities for recycling industrial architecture for new social uses and transforming abandoned materials into playthings, components of the ground or building materials. Permanently closed steel works are preserved while respecting their important testimonial value, and converted to recreational uses "plunged" into an unreal, dialectic natural setting. Since 1983 he is director of the Landscape Architecture department at the University of Munich.

PETER LATZ

53

Landschaftspark,
Duisburg Nord, 1991–99.

Works (a selection) Bürgerpark, Hafeninsel, Saarbrück, 1979–91; Welheimer Mark, Hafeninsel, Saarbrück, 1979–91; Landschaftspark, Duisburg Nord, Germany, 1991–99. **Selected bibliography** *Modern Park Design*, Bussu, 1993; R. Holden, *International Landscape Design*, London, 1996; *Emscher Park, Duisburg in Landscape Trasformed*, London, 1996; P. Latz, *Stadt und Natur-Kunst und Okologie*, Kassel, 1998; *Landschaftpark Duisburg Nord. Okologische und landeskundliche Beiträge*, edited by W. Hoppe and S. Kronsbein, Duisburg, 1999; I. Cortesi, *Il parco pubblico. Paesaggi 1985–2000*, Milan, 2000; *Anthos, Blueprint, Der Architekt, Domus, Landscape Architecture, Remaking Landscape, Stadtbauwelt, Topos, 2G.*

Landschaftspark,
Duisberg Nord, 1991–99.

Ricardo & Victor Legorreta

Mexico

Considered one of Luis Barragán's most accomplished followers, a pupil of José Villagrán García, Ricardo Legorreta is also one of the most famous and prolific Mexican architects. Actually Legorreta has been able to transpose on a larger scale—that includes luxury hotels, resorts, public buildings—Barragán's intimate style, reproducing the details and heightening the contrasting colour range, even turning them into a cliché of "Mexicanness". Ever since his very earliest designs, he has displayed his ability to draw elements from the local tradition and to set up urban areas in keeping with the modernist school, along with a post-modern fondness for scenography. Even in his many gardens Legorreta enhances the elements of the vernacular tradition and those of "poor" architecture—expanses of water, terraces, planted areas, native species—with surrealist gestures meant for the enjoyment of future users. At Solana, near Forth Worth in Texas, in 1990, he planned with Peter Walker a "sublime automobilist experience consisting of bright-coloured posts, long drives separating the surrounding lawns and a cloverleaf inside buttress-walls".

House in Japan,
Zushi, 1998.

Office Building,
Monterrey, 1994.

Office Building,
Monterrey, 1994.

College of Santa Fe Visual Arts Center,
Santa Fe, 1999.

Works (a selection) Automex Chrysler, Toluca, Mexico, 1964; Hotel Camino Real, Mexico City, 1968; Renault Factory, Durango, Mexico, 1984; Solana Westlake-Southlake Campus, Texas, 1988; Marco Museum, Monterrey, Mexico, 1993; Cathedral of Managua, Nicaragua, 1994; San Antonio Main Library, San Antonio, Texas; Office Building, Monterrey, Mexico, 1994; Plaza Reforma, Mexico City; Main Library, University of Nuevo Leon, Monterrey, Mexico, 1995; Renovation of the Colegio de San Ildefonso, Mexico City; Club de Banqueros, Mexico City; Centro Nacional para las Artes, Mexico City, 1995; Amro Bank Corporate Offices, Mexico City, 1996; Schwab Residential Center at Stanford University, Palo Alto, California, 1997; The Tech Museum of Innovation, San José, California, 1998; Ucla Tom Bradley International Hall, Los Angeles, California, 1998; Televisa Corporate Offices, Mexico City, 1998; Telepro Office Building, Mexico City, 1999; College of Santa Fe Visual Arts Center, Santa Fe, New Mexico, 1999; Arizan Office Building, Mexico City, 2000. **Monographs** W. Attoe, *La arquitectura de Ricardo Legorreta*, Mexico, 1990; E. R. Burian, R. Legorreta, *Modernity and the Architecture of Mexico*, Austin (1990), 1997; J. V. Mutlow, *Ricardo Legorreta Architects*, New York, 1997.

Maya Lin

Usa
1959

The Wave Field,
University of Michigan,
Ann Arbor, 1993–95.

Vietnam Veterans Memorial,
Washington, 1982.

A Chinese-born American, in 1981 when still a student at the Yale School of Architecture, she won the competition for the Vietnam Veterans Memorial of Washington. Both in architecture (design for the Museum of African Art in New York, the Mock Sanders Residence in San Francisco) and in memorials (Civil Rights Memorial at Montgomery, Groundswell at the Wexner Center for the Arts at Columbus, and Eclipsed Time at the Pennsylvania Station in New York) she has shown outstanding skill in combining art and architecture and in creating public areas dedicated to remembrance and reflection. The Vietnam Memorial appears like a cleft in the ground, with a long, shiny black stone wall looming out of and sinking into it; a composition that is minimal yet not static, to be interpreted by following its outer perimeter or moving about in the area enclosed by the corner formed by the two walls.

MAYA LIN

55

Works Vietnam Veterans Memorial, Washington, 1982; Civil Rights Memorial, Montgomery, Alabama, 1989; Topo, Charlotte, North Carolina, 1991; Women's Table, Yale University, 1993; The Wave Field, University of Michigan, Ann Arbor, 1993–95; Plaza UC Irwine's School of the Arts, California, 2000–02. **Selected bibliography** M. Lin, *Maya Lin: Public/Private*, Art Publishers, 1994; *Maya Lin*, edited by B. Ling, Milan, 1997.

Richard Long

England
1945

Sculptor, photographer, artist. Ever since the Land Art experiments he performed in Los Angeles between the late sixties and the early seventies, Richard Long has assimilated his artistic activity with the action of walking across natural surroundings, recording with graphics and photographs the action and changes that this has brought about in the environment. Alterations that can be simple gestures (throwing a stone) or the creation of geometric marks produced by repeated coming and going through the same place. A relationship with the surface that has become for the artist the only way he can communicate with the places he walks across: traces, footprints, signs, or even stones slightly displaced or arranged in small or large circles, like in a ritual of worship addressed to nature. In deciding to act in uncontaminated landscapes he expresses his criticism of the separation between nature and culture on which our civilization is grounded, and his striving to restore direct contact with the natural environment. Some of his most famous works, which have even become emblematic of an entire era of artistic experiments, are the large stone circles, geometric shapes formed by an act of the intellect, yet rooted in the organic world.

56

Scirocco Circle,
Island of Pantelleria, 2000.

Crossing Marks,
Sahara, 1988.

Circle of Iceland, 1994.

Catalogues and selected bibliography *Richard Long, Walking in Circles* (Hayward Gallery), London, 1991; *Richard Long, River to River* (Musée d'Art Moderne de la Ville de Paris), Paris, 1993; *Richard Long* (Palazzo delle Esposizioni), Milan, 1994; *Richard Long, Somerset Willow Line*, New York, 1995; *Richard Long, Circles Cycles Mud Stones* (Contemporary Arts Museum), Houston, 1996; *Dolomite Stones, Richard Long* (AR/GE Kunst Galleria Museo), Bolzano, 1996; *Richard Long. From Time to Time*, Cantz, Ostfildern-Ruit, 1997; *Richard Long, Mirage* (Palermo, Cantieri Culturali alla Zisa), Soso (Vicenza), 1997; R. Long, *A Walk across England: A Walk of 382 Miles in 11 Days from the West Coast to the East Coast of England*, New York, 1997; *Land and Environmental Art*, edited by J. Kastner and B. Willis, Hong Kong, 1998.

walking does not belong to me,
these things belong to everyone.

I am interested in using stones as an original material
and in walking in an original way"

M N

ALEX S. MACLEAN

Alex S.
MacLean

Usa

A photographer and pilot, Alex MacLean spent twenty years flying over America in all directions. With one hand on the controls of his airplane and the other on his camera, he caught and recorded spectacular images of what can only be seen from above: the amazing patterns of both the natural environment and man-created landscape. MacLean's aerial photographs frame, select, show, represent an extraordinary sequence of places and bits of territory shot from a height of several hundred metres. Nature and artifice form figures of unforeseen beauty that tell about how the territory is being used—for farming, housing, leisure, transportation, energy production—and only too often abused by deforestation, pollution and exploitation of natural resources. From historical and geographic traces, like the San Andreas fault and the stone walls of New England, to ultramodern shopping centres, low-cost housing, snow-covered baseball fields, MacLean's lens isolates the ordinary and the extraordinary, covering the whole range of patterns and colours composing the rich and variegated American landscape.

Wheat Strips on Plateau,
Cutbank, Montana.

Flower Fields,
Oceanside, California.

Exhibitions "Aerial Perspectives", Lincoln Library, Lincoln, Massachusetts, 1991; "Looking at the Land", The Kathleen Ewing Gallery, Washington, 1993; "Aerial Landscapes", Boston Society of Architects, Boston, Massachusetts, 1993; "Aerial Landscapes", Seaside Institute, Seaside, Florida, 1994. **Selected bibliography** A. MacLean, *Look at the Land: Aerial Reflections on America*, New York, 1993; J. W. Reps, *Cities of the Mississippi: Nineteenth-Century Images of Urban Development*, Columbia, 1994; *Taking Measures Across the American Landscape*, New Haven, 1996.

*Citrus Groves
with Sprinkler Irrigation,*
Blythe, California.

Segmented Field,
Teton River, Montana.

B–52 "Bone Yards",
Davis-Monthan Air Force
Base, Tucson, Arizona.

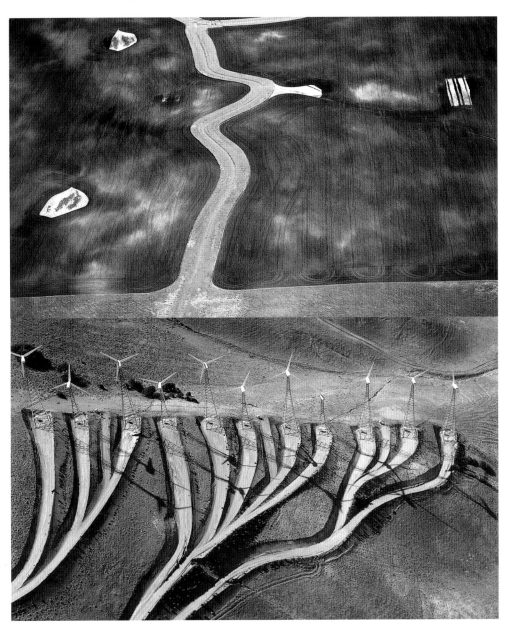

*Logging Raft alongside
Paper Mill*, Bellingham,
Washington.

Field with Tractor Lines,
Munich, North Dakota.

Windmill Row with Roads,
Tehachapi, California.

Shunmyo
Masuno

Japan
1953

A Buddhist monk and assistant monk in the Kenkoh-ji temple, at Yokohama, Shunmyo Masuno studied at the Agriculture Faculty in Tokyo. With Japan Landscape Consultants, founded in 1982, he introduced and brought up to date, not just in Japan, the tradition of zen gardens. True to the principle of the *shakkei*, "the borrowed garden", that symbolically comprises within the garden enclosure remote elements of the landscape, Masuno creates artificial landscapes where rocks, fountains and bushes, even in the most congested urban sites, are endowed with the same suggestiveness as mountains, water-falls and forests. The terraces of the Kohjimachi Kaikan Hotel, in downtown Tokyo, the grounds around the Kagawa Prefectural Library, built in the former airport, or the roof of the Canadian Museum of Civilization, in Ottawa, rather than suggestive gardens are places for meditation and contemplation. Shunmyo Masuno taught at the Tama Art University and is lecturer at the University of British Columbia.

Bathroom Garden,
Art Lake Golf Club,
Nose, 1991.

Kohjimachi Kaikan Hotel,
Tokyo, 1998.

Works Peace Park, Wewak, Papua New Guinea, 1981–82; Nitobe Garden, University of British Columbia, Vancouver, Canada, 1986–93; Tokyo Metropolitan University, Tokyo, 1987–91; Canadian Embassy, Tokyo, 1987–91; Art Lake Golf and Country Club, Osaka, Japan, 1988–91; Kagawa Prefectural Library, Takamatsu, Japan, 1993; Prefectural Museum of Modern Art, Niigata, Japan, 1993; Information-Culture Center, Hanoura, Japan, 1993–95; Plaza for National Research Institute for Metals, Science and Technology Agency, Tsukuba, Japan, 1994; Canadian Museum of Civilization, Ottawa, 1994–95; Garden for Kokusai Hotel, Imabari, Japan, 1996; Letham Grange Hotel & Golf Course, Collison Angus, Scotland, 1996; Kohjimachi Kaikan Hotel, Tokyo, 1998; Courtyard for the Environment Design Department of Tama Art University, Hachioh-ji City, Tokyo, 1998; Denenchofu Park Condominium, Tokyo, 1998; Residential Garden at Gotanda, Tokyo, 1998; Garden for Shiuntai Building in Gion-ji Temple, Mito, Japan, 1999; Back Garden for Rensho-ji Temple, Yokohama, Japan, 1999. **Monographs** *Process Architecture: Landscapes in the Spirit of Zen*, 1995; J. Grayson Trulove, S. Masumo, *Ten Landscapes, Shunmyo Masuno*, Rockport, Massachusetts, 1999.

"Designing gardens is a part of my shugyo"

Garden for Kokusai Hotel,
Imabari, 1996.

Plaza of National
Research Institute for Metals,
Tsukuba, 1994.

Kohjimachi Kaikan Hotel,
Tokyo, 1998.

"Zen thought and Japanese landscaping
are closely bound to one another"

THOMAS MCBROOM

Thomas McBroom

Canada

The Algonquin Golf Course,
St. Andrews by the Sea,
New Brunswick, 2000
(Barrett & MacKay Photo).

Heron Point, Ancaster, 1993.

Paul Desmarais
Golf Course, Murray Bay
(Barrett & MacKay Photo).

Landscaper. Thomas McBroom deals exclusively in planning, designing and creating golf courses in North America. McBroom's work is essentially based on his profound understanding of the history and the tradition of golf combined with a feel for the natural environment. McBroom in fact blends, with distinction, the influence of the great golf course designers with his own vision and particular style. His skill lies in his ability to detect and capture the essence and character of each site, to grasp the natural and geomorphological features of the territory and, in the end, to mesh a golf course into the landscape while protecting the environment as much as possible. His latest works include designs in British Columbia, Ontario, Quebec, Nova Scotia, New Brunswick and Prince Edward Island.

Works (1993–2002) National Pines Golf Course, Barrie, Ontario, 1993; Heron Point, Ancaster, Canada, 1993; Ottawa Hunt, Ottawa, 1993; The Links at Crowbush Cove, Morell, Canada, 1994; Langara, Vancouver, 1994; Morgan Creek, White Rock, British Columbia, 1995; Le Géant, Mont Tremblant, Quebec, 1995; The Lake Joseph Club, Port Sandfield, Ontario, 1996; The Donalda Club, Toronto, 1997; Bell Bay Golf Club, Baddeck, Nova Scotia, 1997; Timberwolf Golf Club, Sudbury, Ontario, 1998; Fraserview, Vancouver, 1998; Rattlesnake Point, Oakville, Canada, 1999; Domaine de la Forêt, Charlesvoix, Quebec, 1999; The Algonquin, St. Andrews by the Sea, New Brunswick, 2000; The Granite Club, Toronto, 2000; King's Riding, Aurora, Canada, 2000; New Niagara Parks Commission Golf Courses, Niagara Falls, Ontario, 2001; The Club at Malpeque Bay, Prince Edward Island, Canada, 2002; Boulder Ridge Golf & Country Club, Collingwood, Canada, 2002.

ENRIC MIRALLES MOYA

Enric Miralles
Moya

Spain
1955-2000

An architect, Enric Miralles won worldwide recognition with two designs created in Barcelona in the early nineties; the archery range in the Olympic district of Vall d'Hebron and the cemetery of Igualada. In both works Miralles associated figures drawn from deconstructionist architecture, references to Antoni Gaudí, methods and materials inspired by Arte Povera. The outcome is a transposition of architecture in an unusual landscape dimension, in which the materials—stone, concrete, oxidized iron—are associated with earthworks to build a contemporary garden. Recently passed away, he taught at the Architecture School of Barcelona as of 1985, at the Stadelschule of Frankfurt as of 1992. He was Visiting Professor in the leading architecture schools, including Columbia University, Princeton University, Rio de Janeiro and Mexico City, the Berlage Institute and the Mackintosh School.

60

Igualada Cemetery,
Barcelona, 1985–92
(with Carme Pinós).

Works La Llauna School Building, Badalona, Spain; Igualada Cemetery, Barcelona, 1985–92 (with Carme Pinós); Archery Range, Barcelona, 1987–92 (with Carme Pinós); Dance School and Indoor Stadium, Alicante, Spain, 1989–93; Icaria Avenue Pergolas, Barcelona, 1990–92; Entrance Area, Takaoka Station, Japan, 1991–93; Unazuki Pavilion, Japan, 1991–93; Sports Facility, Huesca, Spain, 1992–94. **Selected bibliography** B. Tagliabue Miralles, *Enric Miralles. Works and Projects 1975–1995*, New York-Milan, 1996; *Abitare, Architectural Record, Architectural Review, Architektur, Arquitectura Viva, Bauwelt, Casabella, Daidaios, Domus, GA Document, L'Architecture d'aujourd'hui, L'Architettura, Progressive Architecture, Quaderns d'arquitectura i urbanisme, Topos.*

MARY MISS

Mary Miss

Usa

1944

The work of Mary Miss bears upon the construction of urban areas of our times, associating art, design, archaeology, landscape architecture and town planning. Her art is not merely restricted to decorating the surface of the landscape by introducing elements, but instead overturns, twists, and re-forms the territory, seeking to provoke an emotional experience. Excavation in fact creates a break, a point of tension, an alteration of the territory that is turned into a form giving rise to a sense of space, not asserted but suggested. Her creations—structures, filters, frames, sequences, using mostly natural materials—become the tool whereby the observer is given the opportunity to focus his attention on a natural vista of a specific place. Her interventions invite the viewers to participate, recognizing the strata and the history of a site by walking in it and going across it, observing it from different points of view and sitting down at different levels to "read" its topography. Not just an emotional involvement, but physical as well, emphasized by the circuits suggested by the dynamic and "open" forms of her installations or the choreographic character of some of the works.

Battery Park, *South Cove*,
New York, 1988.

*Perimeters, Pavilions,
Decoys*, Nassau County
Museum Rosalyn,
New York, 1977–80.

Field Rotation,
Governor's State University,
Park Forest South, Illinois,
1980–81.

University Hospital,
Washington, 1986–90.

Works Battery Park City Landfill, New York, 1973; Perimeters, Pavilions, Decoys, Nassau County Museum Rosalyn, New York, 1977–80; Veiled Landscape, Lake Placid, New York, 1979; Staged Gates, Dayton, Ohio, 1979; Mirror Way, Fogg Museum, Harvard University, Cambridge, Massachusetts, 1980; Field Rotation, Governor's State University, Park Forest South, Illinois, 1980–81; Pool Complex: Orchard Valley, Laumeier Sculpture Park, St. Louis, Missouri, 1982–85; Battery Park, South Cove, New York, 1984–88; Arrivals and Departures: 100 Doors, Dallas Museums, Dallas, Texas, 1986; University Hospital, Seattle, Washington, 1986–90; Hayden Square, Tempe, Arizona, 1987; Des Moines Art Center, Des Moines, Iowa, 1989–96; Rutgers University, New Brunswick, New Jersey, 1992–94; Jyvaskyla, Finland, 1994; University of Houston Athletic/Alumni Facility, Houston, Texas, 1995–97; Ladder for a Beech Tree, Neuberger Museum, SUNY Purchase, New York, 1999; 14th Street Union Square Subway Station, New York, 1999; Milwaukee Riverwalk, Milwaukee, Wisconsin, 1999. **Selected bibliography** *The American Landscape, Christian Zapatka*, edited by M. Zardini, New York, 1996; *Land and Environmental Art*, edited by J. Kastner and B. Willis, Hong Kong, 1998.

"I have investigated the creation of places that are open and accessible while at the same time providing breathing space; here, the interior life of the individual can be considered"

ROBERT K. MURASE

Robert K. Murase

Usa
1938

Japanese American Historical Plaza, Portland, Oregon.

A third-generation Japanese American, at the start of his career Robert Murase worked in the studios of Robert Royston and Lawrence Halprin, and to enrich his experience he then worked in Japan. With over thirty years of experience as a landscape architect, Murase has designed courtyards and outdoor areas for museums, libraries, hospitals, schools and public buildings. He is also responsible for the site planning and designing of resorts and tourist complexes, university campuses, parks and recreation equipment. Murase's gardens combine features of the American tradition with other ones from Japan, as in the case of the famous stone and water garden for the new pavilion of the Japanese American National Museum. He has worked all over the world, including the United States, Japan, the Pacific archipelagos and the Caribbean islands. His latest works are the design for the Borobudur Archaeological Center and for the Prambanan Temple in Indonesia; the master plan for the Seattle Center Waterfront; the Wilsonville Town Center in Oregon; the development plan of the Goshogaware Civic Core District; and the Benaroya Concert Hall Garden of Remembrance in Seattle.

ROBERT K. MURASE

62

Works (a selection) Borobudur Archaeological Center and Prambanan Temple Landscape, Indonesia; Port of Seattle Pier 69, Seattle, Washington; Wilsonville Town Center Park, Oregon; Goshogaware Civic Core District; Benaroya Concert Hall Garden of Remembrance, Seattle, Washington; Collins Circle, Portland, Oregon; Stone and Water Garden, Japanese American National Museum, Los Angeles, California; Tanner Creek Park, Portland, Oregon; Japanese American Historical Plaza, Portland, Oregon. **Selected bibliography** G. Cooper, G. Taylor, *Paradise Transformed. The Private Garden for the Twenty-First Century*, New York, 1996; M. Leccese, *Robert Murase. Stone and Water*, Washington, 1997; J. Beardsley, *Earthworks and Beyond*, New York, 1998; *Designed Landscape Forum 1*, edited by G. Crandell and E. Reifeiss, Washington, 1998; *100 Years of Landscape Architecture: Some Patterns of a Century*, edited by M. Simo, Washington, 1999; M. Leccese, *American Eden. Landscape Architecture of the Pacific West*, Paris, 2000.

Collins Circle,
Portland, Oregon.

Myodo Kyo Kai,
Shiga Prefecture.

Garden of Remembrance,
Seattle, Washington.

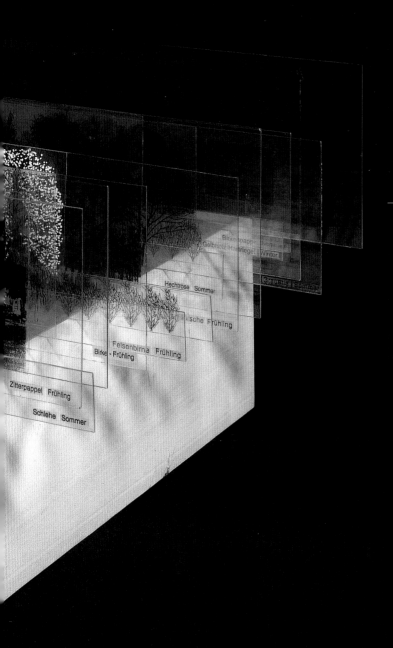

OP

Laurie Olin

Usa

1934

Laurie Olin is a landscaper who grew up in Alaska, in one of the last great natural landscapes. He trained as an architect at the University of Washington, and lived and worked in Seattle, New York, London and Philadelphia. For Olin city landscapes are a design challenge as well as an opportunity to recreate landscapes just as wild as natural ones. However, the spaces and the structures thus created, so "ecologically" different, appear poised in suspension, at times even too socially correct or spiritually functional. In 1980 he began designing in the United States and Great Britain for institutions, large-scale city projects and public areas with SOM, Norman Foster, Cooper Robertson and Frank Gehry, Peter Eisenman. He has spent the past ten years restoring parks and public areas in New York, Rome, Houston and Philadelphia while still collaborating with architects, including Ricardo Legorreta, Richard Meier and Stephen Holl for public

plazas, museums and schools. In 1974 he became a faculty member at the University of Pennsylvania, where he presently teaches, after being chairman of the Landscape Architecture Department of Harvard from 1982 to 1987.

63

LAURIE OLIN

Wagner Park,
New York.

National Gallery of Art Sculpture Garden,
Washington.

Cactus Garden,
J. Paul Getty Center,
Los Angeles, California.

Bryant Park
Restoration, New York
(MacLean Photo).

Vila Olimpica,
Barcelona.

Works (a selection) Westlake Park, Seattle, Washington; Wagner Park, New York; Vila Olimpica, Barcelona; Playa Vista, Los Angeles, California; Wexner Center for the Arts, Ohio State University, Columbus, Ohio; National Gallery of Art Sculpture Garden, Washington; Goldstein Development, Frankfurt am Main; J. Paul Getty Center, Los Angeles, California; 16th Street Transitway/Mall, Denver, Colorado; Bryant Park, New York; Exchange Square – Bishopsgate, London; Battery Park City Esplanade, New York; American Academy in Rome, Rome; Independence National Historical Park, Philadelphia. **Selected bibliography** J. Dixon Hunt, P. Rowe, *Transforming the Common Place. Selections from Laurie Olin's Sketchbooks,* Cambridge, Mass., 1997; J. W. Thompson, *The Rebirth of Bryant Park,* Washington, 1997; L. Olin, *Across the Open Fields. Essays Drawn from English Landscapes,* Philadelphia, 1999. He is the author of several essays published in *Arcade, Forces, GSD News, Journal of Garden Design History, Landscape Design, Landscape Journal, Landscape Architecture, Places, The Design Book Review.*

"The landscape is one of the least understood
and most complex products of society:
its design can and should be
among the highest of the arts"

ROBERTO PIRZIO BIROLI

Roberto
Pirzio Biroli

Italy
1942

Pirzio Biroli's work, among his many professional interests, also involves designing parks and city gardens, that he considers requalifying factors for suburban areas. In 1994, along the course of the Cormor River, concerning a two-thousand hectares area on the outskirts of Udine, he suggested rebuilding and transforming an abandoned farming area, now become a blighted part of the city. After reclaiming the area by improving the countless dumps with landfill, he created small lookout points and water pools or tumuli or other figures belonging to the Western garden tradition; with new avenues and canals and by consolidating the slopes with new planting he was able to "put back in order" even the vistas onto the surrounding countryside. Last, he built a small pavilion, inspired by the one Heinrich Tessenov designed in 1936 for the island of Rügen. He was Visiting Professor at Berkeley and Potsdam, and presently teaches at the University of Lubeck and the Polytechnic of Zurich.

64

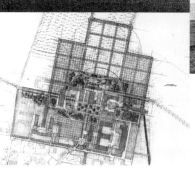

Cormor Park,
Udine, 1994.

Lennésche Feldur,
Potsdam, 1995–.

Works Cormor Park, Udine, Italy, 1994; Public Park, Lubeck; Lennésche Feldur, Potsdam, Germany, 1995–. **Selected bibliography** P. Portoghesi, *I nuovi architetti italiani*, Rome, 1983; P. Portoghesi, *Postmodern*, New York, 1983; I. Cortesi, *Il parco pubblico. Paesaggi 1985–2000*, Milan, 2000. His works have been published in the reviews *Abitare, Bauwelt, Costruire, Daidalos, L'Architecture d'aujourd'hui, Lotus international, Materia, Parametro, Phalaris, Progressive Architecture*.

LINDA POLLAK

Linda Pollak

Usa
1954

Roof Terrace, Manhattan,
New York, 1992–93.

*Hell's Kitchen South,
"Islands" and "Bridges"*,
Javits Center Park,
New York, 1999.

On her own or else in collaboration with Sandro Marpillero, Linda Pollak explores how issues relating to spatial differences have bearing on architectural, landscape and urban space design, always starting from the premise that each place inevitably belongs to a multiple range of activities. Interaction between different types of information actually helps identify situations in which a limited intervention can achieve far greater urban and ecological repercussions. Her ability to alter factors that were historically attributed to different disciplines accounts for designs that move in more than one direction—toward city and nature, toward detail and context. She is the author of a recent publication about public areas, and presently teaches at the Harvard Graduate School of Design.

LINDA POLLAK

65

Works Drawing on Site, Reclamation Park, Charles River Dam, Boston, Massachusetts, 1990; Roof Terrace, 500 Park Avenue, Manhattan, New York, 1992–93; Eib's Pond Park, Staten Island, New York, 1998–2000; Jacob Riis Houses Community Center Renovation/Addition, New York, 1999–2000; Harlem RBI: Little League Baseball Park, New York, 1999–2000. **Selected bibliography** *Designed Landscape Forum 1*, edited by G. Crandell and E. Reifeiss, Washington, 1998; L. Pollak, A. Berrizbeitia, *Inside Outside. Between Architecture and Landscape*, New York, 2000; *Archis, Casabella, Daidalos, Domain, Harvard Design Magazine, Interior Design Magazine, Modulus 25, Oculus*.

REGINA POLY

Regina Poly

Germany

A pupil of Oswald Matthias Ungers at the University of Berlin, Regina Poly interprets the garden theme according to a Cartesian or strictly geometrical compositional score, combining the favourite motifs of American landscaping—in particular Peter Walker's—with ones that more clearly belong to the German school. On the one hand, she imposes abstract geometric compositions consisting of plant elements associated with the graphic treatment of paved surfaces; on the other, in an apparent contradiction, she lends close attention to urban features and the site's possible natural tendencies, the latter resolved by introducing particular tree species. Her gardens either look like new urban areas, oases contrasted with the buildings, or like urban furnishings, flowerbeds or spots of greenery, without the least reference to nature. In this second aspect, Poly's Berlin works seek to mark or shape anew the organization of outdoor areas, coinciding with programmes that engaged the city after its reunification, and that range from interventions on the territorial scale, with the reclamation of abandoned industrial areas, to revitalization of blighted urban areas.

*Innenhof
Charlottenburger Ufer*,
Berlin, 1988
(Reinhard Photo).

Works City Park S. Chiara, Trento, Italy, 1983–89; Theodor-Wolff-Park, Friedrichstrasse, Berlin, 1985–90; Innenhof Charlottenburger Ufer, Berlin, 1987–88; Wohnumfeldverbesserung Loschwitzer Weg, Berlin Spandau, 1988–90; Villengarten am Wannsee, Berlin, 1991–96; Vorplatz und Garten des neuen Abgeordnetenhauses, Berlin, 1992–93; Gartenanlage der Wohnbebauung Lehrter-Perleberger Strasse, Berlin, 1993–96; Innenhof und Strassenraum des Art Center und Art Hotel, Dresden, 1994–96; Dorfplatz in Ketzin, Brandenburg, 1995–97; Innenhöfe und Garten des Bundesministerium der Finanzen, Berlin, 1995–2000; Gartenanlage Falkenseer Chaussee, Berlin Spandau, 1997; Regelwerk zu den Aussenanlagen des WISTA-Geländes, Berlin Adlershof, 1998–99 (with K. Laube and E.-M. Schön); Gartenhof des Seniorenwohnheimes Passauer Strasse 5-7, Berlin, 1998–99; Tuchollaplatz in Berlin Lichtenberg Bauherr: Bezirksamt Lichtenberg, 1999; Auswahlverfahren zur Gestaltung des Freiraumes zwischen den alten Kasernengebäuden und Neubauten für die Humboldt Universität, Berlin Adlershof, 1999–2000; Neugestaltung des Schulhofes des Canisius Kollegs, Tiergarten, 1999–2000. **Selected bibliography** *Regina Poly - Plätze, Innenhöfe, Parkanlagen 1985–1998*, Cologne, 1998; *Bauwelt, Stadt Bauwelt*.

*Bundesministerium
der Finanzen,*
Berlin, 1995–2000
(T. Bruns Photo).

*Vorplatz und Garten
des neuen Abgeordnetenhauses,*
Berlin, 1992–93
(Reinhard Photo).

ELIOT PORTER

Eliot Porter

Usa
1901-1990

Green Algae, Mombasa,
Kenya, 22 October 1970.

Pahoehoe Lava,
James Island, Galapagos,
10 March 1966.

Photographer. Eliot Porter was one of the most famous contemporary American photographers of nature; his images represent particular situations and moments of the natural world by a use of colour that is the truest possible to the original, achieved through a particular, innovatory process that clearly distinguishes from the tones black and white photography produces. Trained as a biochemist, his colour photographs always reflect his desire to study the natural environment from close-up and his fascination for the development and adaptation of fauna and flora to their habitat. His point of view is frequently on ground level and reminds us of the image of the botanist looking for exemplars and rare scientific items. His work on Greece, the Antarctic, China, Maine and on North American birds has appeared in a number of books and exhibition catalogues.

Selected bibliography *In Wildness Is the Preservation of the World,* San Francisco, 1962; *Summer Island: Penobscot Country,* edited by D. Brower, San Francisco, 1966; *Forever Wild: the Adirondacks. Photos,* New York, 1966; *Baja California and the Geography of Hope,* San Francisco, 1967; *Appalachian Wilderness. The Great Smoky Mountains,* New York, 1970; *Intimate Landscapes: Photographs,* New York, 1979; *American Places,* edited by J. Macrae III, New York, 1981; *All under Heaven: the Chinese World,* New York, 1983; *Eliot Porter's Southwest,* New York, 1985; *Maine / Eliot Porter,* Boston, 1986; *Eliot Porter Photographs and Texts,* Boston, 1987; *Mexican Churches,* Albuquerque, 1987; *The Place No One Knew: Glen Canyon on the Colorado,* Layton, 1988 (San Francisco, 1966); *The West,* Boston, 1988; *Iceland,* Boston, 1989; *Nature's Chaos,* New York, 1990.

Dead Leaves,
Red River Gorge, Kentucky,
19 April 1968.

Wave-Worn Rock,
Hellnar, Snaefellsnes,
14 July 1972.

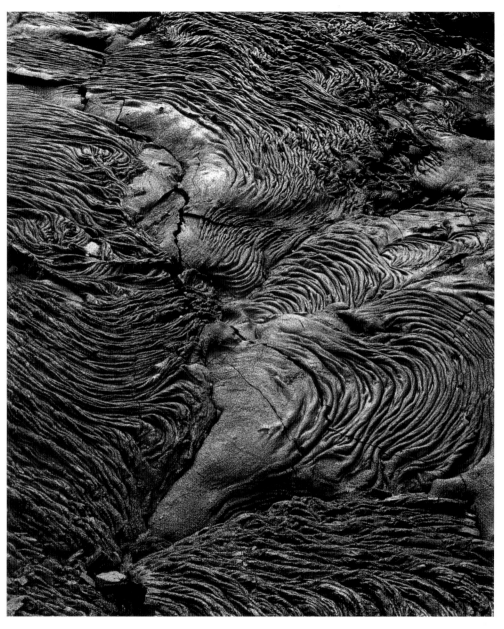

Gumbo Limbo Bark,
Everglades National Park,
Florida, 24 February 1974.

Lava Flow,
James Island, Galapagos,
10 March 1966.

Tanya Preminger

Israel
[Russia]

1944

Sculptor. Tanya Preminger, a Russian artist emigrated to Israel, works essentially with natural materials, such as earth, grass and stone, using and freely applying various artistic techniques and experiments: sculpture, Land Art, installations and photography. She has had several one-man shows in Israel and taken part in over forty exhibitions in Israel, Russia, Japan, Korea, the United States and Europe. In the works she makes using earth and plants, like *Boiling*, *Balance* and *Beyond Fairway*, Preminger creates gardens and invents elements whose clarity and figurative immediacy are fused with an intense symbolic and evocative power. The symbolic form of the garden allows her to create images that touch on the most intimate parts of our consciousness, and that refer to the body, sexuality, and the secret, vital bond we have with the earth.

Screen, Hazoz
Haglilit City, 1996.

Balance, Kibbutz
Givat-Brener, 1989.

Boiling, 1988.

*Window into Another
World*, Kibbutz
Givat-Brener, 1989.

Hades, 1991.

One-man shows Leivik House, Tel Aviv, 1978; Ramat Gan Museum, Israel, 1984; Zvi Noam Art Gallery, Tel Aviv, 1985, Sharet Gallery, Givatayim, 1987; Herzliya Museum, Israel, 1988; Efrat Gallery, Tel Aviv, 1989; "Sculpture in the grass", Givat-Brener, 1989; Negev Museum, Beersheba, 1990; Tova Osman Gallery, Tel Aviv, 1990; "Urban Sculpture", Ra'anana, 1990; "Some Works", Tova Osman Gallery, Tel Aviv, 1991; "Photography", Tova Osman Gallery, Tel Aviv, 1993; "Stone Works", Arsoof Gallery, Rishpon, 1993; "Rolling Stones", Tova Osman Gallery, Tel Aviv, 1995; Lutshansky Museum, Givat-Brener, 1995; "At Home", Artists House, Jerusalem, 1996; Efrat Gallery, Tel Aviv, 1997. **Selected bibliography** *Tanya Preminger*, Negev Museum, Beersheba, 1990; *Tanya Preminger: Works 1984–1994*, Tel Aviv, 1994; *Tanya Preminger 1995–1997*, Arsuf, 1997; *Land and Environmental Art*, edited by J. Kastner and B. Willis, Hong Kong, 1998; *Mile Stones*, The Open Museum, Tefen, 1998; *The Exhibition of Contemporary Sculpture*, Miyazaki, 2000; *Designed Landscape Forum*, Washington, 2000.

ALAIN PROVOST

Alain Provost

France
1938

Alain Provost is a landscape architect and horticultural engineer. His curriculum is truly impressive: it includes the André Citroën park in Paris, the rehabilitation of the Roissy airport, the La Courneuve park (Seine-Saint-Denis), without omitting his designs for the banks of the Rhone River at Lyon. Multiple approaches and different solutions that occasionally even clash are characteristic of his work, whether he is treating, even on the same scale, gardens, parks or entire areas. For the La Courneuve park he designed over 400 hectares of undulating forms that blend in with the wooded hills, lakes and lawns. On the other hand, his designs for blighted industrial areas in Paris are strictly Cartesian, whereas at the Parc Floral water is the factor that organizes space. But, beyond their most obvious differences, Provost's designs always express concern for the introduction of new interventions in the context, that paradoxically he even proceeds to invent, combining his designing skill with his botanical expertise.

ALAIN PROVOST

69

André Citroën Park,
Paris, 1986–92.

Diderot Park, Paris,
La Défense, 1981–92.

Works Jardin des Plantes Aquatiques du Parc Floral, Paris, 1969; Parc de la Préfecture, Cergy-Pontoise, 1972–74; Parc de La Courneuve, Seine-Saint-Denis, France, 1972–2000; Traversée du Périphérique dans le Bois de Boulogne, 1974; Parc Diderot, Paris La Défense, 1981–92; Jardins des Présidences de la République du Cameroun et du Gabon, 1982–89; Parc André Citroën, Paris, 1986–92; Eurotunnel, Calais, 1987; Rives du Rhône, Lyon, 1991–2000; Renault Technocentre, Guyancourt, France, 1992–2000; Autoroutes A14 and A20, Brive-Montauban, 1995–2000; Thames Barrier Park, London 1995–2000; Ring de l'Aéroport de Roissy, 1995–2000. **Selected bibliography** *André Citroën Park*, edited by F. Cerver, Barcelona, 1994; I. Cortesi, *Il parco pubblico. Paesaggi 1985–2000*, Milan, 2000; *Lotus international*, *Pages Paysages*, *Topos*.

Béarn Park, Saint-Cloud.   *Renault Technocentre*,
Guyancourt, 1992–2000.

RS

Douglas Reed

Usa

Landscape architect. Douglas Reed won international acclaim for his design of the Therapeutic Garden for Children created near Boston for a care centre for children with behavioural problems. The Therapeutic Garden becomes an extraordinarily appropriate medium for telling—in direct, symbolic or allegorical terms—the story of the stages of disease and recovery. These stages coincide with a sequence of areas connected by a stream running through the site. In fact, by topographic remodelling Reed designed a cave-shelter (safety), a wooded, mountainous area (exploring), a small hill for climbing (difficulty), an island for playing alone, a pond (discovery), steep shallow slopes as a challenge, and a large lawn for playing. Water is the principal unifying element of the design, flowing from the terrace and then into the stream that winds its way through the garden—symbolizing, as in every garden, life. The stream is actually a small artificial canal, twenty centimetres wide with metal banks and pebbles on the bottom.

Therapeutic Garden for Children, Wellesley, Massachusetts, 1996.

Works South Cove, New York, 1988 (with M. Miss and S. Child); Grand Isle Residence, Lake Champlain, Vermont, 1988–91 (with S. Child); Garden, Richmond, Massachusetts, 1989 (with S. Child and T. Mitani); Family Cemetery, Troy, Ohio, 1990, (with S. Child); Esplanade Roof Terrace, Cambridge, Massachusetts, 1991 (with S. Child and T. Mitani); Nantucket Island Residence, Massachusetts, 1992 (with S. Child); Carl Shapiro, Beth Israel Hospital, Boston, Massachusetts, 1996 (with S. Child); Therapeutic Garden for Children, Wellesley, Massachusetts, 1996. **Selected bibliography** *Designed Landscape Forum 1*, edited by G. Crandell and E. Reifeiss, Washington, 1998; *100 Years of Landscape Architecture: Some Patterns of a Century*, edited by M. Simo, Washington, 1999; G. Cooper, G. Taylor, *Gardens for the Future*, New York, 2000; *Art New England*, *Garden Design*, *Landscape Architecture*.

REISER + UMEMOTO

Jesse Reiser
Nanako Umemoto

Usa

Japan

The Reiser + Umemoto studio has devoted the past ten years to large-scale urban infrastructures, such as, for instance, the designs for the Croton Aqueduct in New York State (1990), for the East River in Manhattan (1998–99) and the competition for the west side of Manhattan sponsored by the International Foundation for the Canadian Center for Architecture. Cities are the main link between flows of material and information, that in time developed in countless transportation, distribution, cultural and educational facilities. Increasingly obvious worldwide interconnections have produced cities where global systems are integrated in local environments and where you transit swiftly from a local dimension to a regional or international one. So each of their designs aims at unifying environments hitherto separated, by constantly investigating the relationships between architecture, communication systems and territory, so that the city of the twenty-first century will be able to bear with these urban interconnections and find itself a new form. Jesse Reiser and Nanako Umemoto have been working together since 1986 as Reiser + Umemoto.

Wolf Residence,
Sands Point,
New York, 1998.

J. Jadow Residence,
Mill River,
Massachusetts, 1997.

Works (a selection) Croton Aqueduct Study, New York, 1990; Project for the Porto di Venezia, Biennial of Architecture, Venice, 1990; East River Corridor Manhattan, New York, 1998–99; Hudson River Park RFQ, New York, 2000 (with E. Norten); Unicare Headquarters, Sarasota, Florida, 2000.
Selected bibliography A. Benjamin, *Reiser + Umemoto Recent Projects*, London, 1998; *Abitare, Academy Editions, A+U, Archimade, Architectural Design, Architectural Record, Architecture and Urbanism, Architecture Magazine, Assemblage* (Cambridge, Ma.), *Daidalos, Lotus international, Space Design.*

Hudson River Park RFQ,
New York, 2000
(with E. Norton).

Martha Schwartz

Usa
1951

A pupil of Peter Walker, in 1979 she drew worldwide attention with her design for the Bagel Garden in Boston. In her works she has succeeded in combining the stances of Land Art with the creation of functionally useful public areas. Martha Schwartz thus launched an entirely new dimension for designing urban landscape, making the vacant space of the city become a space for art and sculpture, for gardens and architecture. Public areas appear as a new field for cultural action, offering eloquent places and moments that make lingering or crossing through meaningful experiences. Her works, which seek to heighten the expressivity of the context and to communicate the aims of her designs by the "distorsion" of familiar images and/or by using them out of context, are "accessible" even to large numbers. Instead in private gardens Martha Schwartz obviously seeks to associate art and nature by creating sculpture-gardens—like the one in Santa Fe—that

do not merge with the context, but that by a network of fountains and little canals, by the geometrization imposed on the trees constitute an authentic artistic invention.

Davis Garden,
El Paso, Texas, 1994.

Littman Wedding,
Deal, New Jersey, 1995.

Works (a selection) Bagel Garden, Boston, 1979; Whitehead Institute Splice Garden, Cambridge, Massachusetts, 1986; Center for Innovative Technology, Fairfax, Virginia, 1988; Turf Parterre Garden, Battery Park City, New York, 1988; Marina Linear Park, San Diego, California, 1988; The Citadel, City of Commerce, California, 1991; Dickenson Garden, Santa Fe, New Mexico, 1991; Kempinski Hotel Park, Munich, Germany, 1992–93; Jacob Javitz Plaza, New York, 1992–96; Davis Garden, El Paso, Texas, 1994; Miami International Airport Sound Attenuation Wall, Miami, Florida, 1996; Kitagata Garden, Gifu, Japan, 1996–99; Spoleto Festival, Charleston, South Carolina, 1997; US Courthouse Plaza, Minneapolis, Minnesota, 1997; Hud Plaza Improvements, Washington, 1998; Power Lines, Landschaftspark Mechtenberg, Gelsenkirchen, Germany, 1999; Exchange Square, Manchester, Great Britain, 2000. **Selected bibliography** G. Cooper, G. Taylor, *Paradise Transformed. The Private Garden for the Twenty-First Century*, New York, 1996; U. Weilacher, *Between Landscape Architecture and Land Art*, Berlin-Basel-Boston, 1996; H. Landecker, E. K. Meyer, *Martha Schwartz: trasfiguration of the Commonplace*, Washington, 1997; J. Beardsley, *Art and Landscape. In Charleston and the Low Country*, Washington, 1998.

Exchange Square,
Manchester, 2000.

Jacob Javits Plaza,
New York, 1996.

"Landscape is a cultural image, a pictorial way of
This may be represented in a variety of materials
in writing on paper, in earth, stone, water,
between two disciplines, contemporary art

epresenting, structuring or symbolizing surroundings…
and on many surfaces—in paint, on canvas,
and vegetation on the ground. I occupy the territory
and landscape architecture"

Hud Plaza,
Washington, 1998.

Splice Garden,
Whitehead Institute,
Cambridge,
Massachusetts, 1986.

*Gifu Kitagata
Apartments*, Gifu, 1999.

Kazuyo Sejima
& Ryue Nishizawa

Japan
1956 and 1966

Sejima graduated in architecture in 1979 at the Japan Woman's University and worked in Toyo Ito's studio from 1981 to 1987. Some of her architectural works are considered examples of the most radical minimalism, designed with intentionally limited formal expressions that aim less at a contemplative character than a throbbing dimension, created by light, reflections, signs and motion. However Sejima does not feel she is a follower of minimalism, although at times she cannot do without a geometrical order, nor is her architecture tempted by avant-garde aspirations. A light outer envelope surrounds several receptacles, creating ambiguous areas rather than accurately distinguishing inside from outside. Her delicate structures, of great technical and formal distinction, seem to belong utterly to the natural suggestiveness of the context in which they are created. Inside areas occasionally suggest the kind of space you usually find outside, and mere membranes separate inside and outside in a semi-permeable way, like airy confines that, thanks to the lighting, become translucent. She has been working with Ryue Nishizawa since 1995.

SEJIMA & NISHIZAWA

73

M House,
Tokyo, 1996–97.

O-Museum,
Lida, Nagano, 1999.

Works (a selection) Housing Platform I, Katsuura, 1987–88; Housing Platform II, Yamanashi, 1988–90; Saishunkan Seiyaku Women's Residence, Kumamoto, 1990–91; Pachinko Parlor I, Hitachi, 1991–93; Villa in the Woods, Chino, 1992–94; Pachinko Parlor II, Naka, 1993; Police Station, Chofu, Tokyo, 1993–94; Pachinko Parlor III, Hitachiohta, 1995; Multimedia Workshop, Oogaki, 1995–96; House S, Okayama, 1995–96; N-Museum, Nakahechi, 1995–97; M House, Tokyo, 1996–97; O-Museum, Lida, Nagano, 1999; Day Care Center, Yokohama, 2000; City of Girls, 7th International Biennial of Architecture, Venice, 2000; Prada Beauty, Shinjuku-ku, Tokyo, 2000; Stadstheater, Almere, Netherlands, 2000. **Selected bibliography** *Architectural Review, Assemblage, Casabella, Daidalos, El Croquis, GA Document, L'Architecture d'aujourd'hui, Lotus international, Lotus navigator, Quaderns d'arquitectura i urbanisme, Space Design, Techniques & Architecture, The Japan Architect.*

O-Museum,
Lida, Nagano, 1999.

Multimedia Workshop,
Oogaki, Gifu, 1995–96.

VLADIMIR SITTA

Vladimir Sitta

Czech Republic

Fire Line/Convergences,
Sydney, 1998.

The Tilt, Garangula,
New South Wales, 1989.

He left Czechoslovakia in 1979, moving to Germany and, since 1981, to Australia. Sitta's gardens arise as a precise response to modern life, and to successfully express their objectives they must be intricately associated with the surrounding context. Modern life itself is the very reason for gardens: the need to find "a personal refuge from the insults gathered in everyday liaisons with practicalities of human survival". Sitta's gardens always come back to the theme of eternity—ephemeral and anarchical—and time is a recurrent theme in his designs. "Time resents any attempt of its appropriation yet it is capable of universally responding to the contemporary human condition.

Nature will always trespass into gardens. Coupled with time they both will offer the unsolicited commentary on our intention."

Theatre of Lights,
Sydney, 1995.

Walled Garden,
Sydney, 1999.

Walk on Water,
Sydney, 1999.

Projects (a selection) Theme Park, Taiwan, 1989; Garangula Private Polo Club, Australia, 1990; Crystal Cathedral Entertainment Complex, Singapore, 1990; Agro-Tourism Complex, Bogor, Indonesia, 1990; Playground Equipment Concept, Kansas City, 1991; City Square, Brno, Czech Republic, 1992; Slavic Square, Brno, Czech Republic, 1993; Urban Paradise, A Proposal for the Urban Garden, New York, 1993; Sydney Olympic Games, Homebush Bay, Urban Design Studio, Australia, 1994; Penfold's Magill Estate Winery, Adelaide, Australia, 1994; Modular Urban Furniture, Frydek-Mistek, Czech Republic, 1994; Greening of Engineering Structures, A Proposal for "Green Tile", Paris, 1994; Peace Square, Prague, Czech Republic, 1994; Macquarie Place, Sydney, 1995; Curiosity Garden, 4th Festival International des Jardins, Chaumont-sur-Loire, France, 1995; Honeysuckle, Newcastle, Australia, 1996; Mendel Square Urban Design and Traffic Concept, Brno, Czech Republic, 1996; Boundary Street Apartments, Sydney, 1998; Giba Park, Sydney, 1998; Redleaf Woollahra Municipal Council, Sydney, 1998; Docklands Esplanade, Melbourne, 1999; Docklands Gateways, Melbourne, 1999; Convention Center, Nanning, China, 1999; Kia Ora Stud Redevelopment, Scone, Australia, 2000; Le Saunier Neuf, Country Estate, France, 2000. **Selected bibliography** H. Edquist, *The Culture of Landscape Architecture,* Melbourne, 1994; S. Cantor, *Contemporary Trends in Landscape Architecture,* New York, 1996; G. Cooper, G. Taylor, *Paradise Transformed, The Private Garden for the Twenty-First Century,* New York, 1996; J. Baskin, T. Dixon, *Australia's Timeless Gardens,* Canberra, 1996; C. Bradley-Hole, *The Minimalist Garden,* London, 1999.

"Nature is a perennial source of fascination. As our cities are becoming increasingly denatured, gardens initiate both our communion with nature and our disjunction, they are often the only entity available for this"

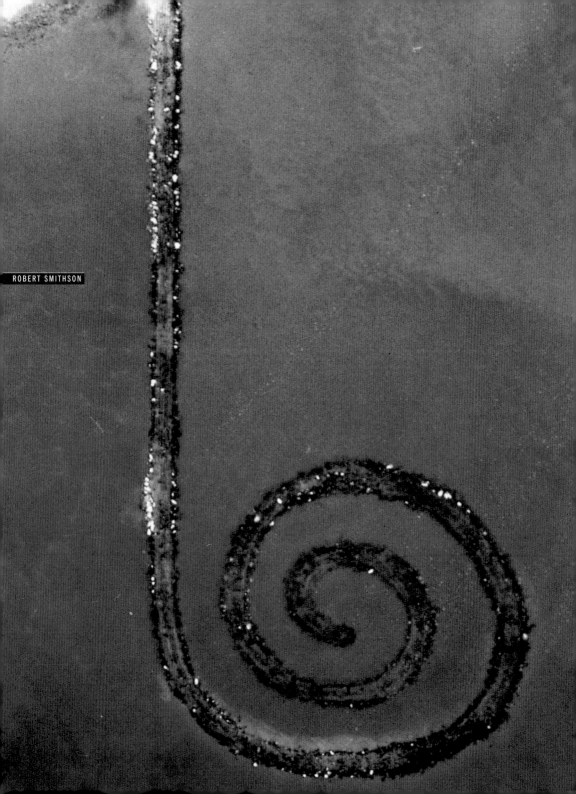

ROBERT SMITHSON

Robert
Smithson

Usa
1938-1973

He is one of the founders of the art form known as Earthworks or Land Art. He owes his worldwide fame essentially to his provocative work, Spiral Jetty, created in 1970 and inspired by the Great Serpent Mound, an Indian monument in Ohio, that expresses open criticism of the art world. Smithson's works define a new, original concept of landscape. The intervention on nature and in nature no longer has an aesthetic and decorative objective; in the works there is no attempt to imitate, emulate or subjugate nature, but that of being integrated, beginning with the very order of nature and using the same available materials, and discovering that natural phenomena in themselves can constitute artistic events when they are isolated, decontextualized. In his "site/non-site" designs in the late sixties and the early seventies, Smithson pointed out some essential theoretic guidelines on the theme of landscape. The places he chose were lakes, dumps and areas ruined by buildings, industrial by-products. From these barren terrains he gathered suggestive fragments—stones, salt cristals, samples of tar—that can be transformed in non-places, abstract mementos of the henceforth missing place.

Spiral Jetty,
Rozel Point,
Great Salt Lake,
Utah, 1970.

Earthworks Asphalt Rundown, Rome, Italy, 1969; Glue Pour, Vancouver, Canada, 1969; Partially Buried Woodshed, Kent, Ohio, 1970; Spiral Jetty, Rozel Point, Great Salt Lake, Utah, 1970; Broken Circle, Emmen, Netherlands, 1971; Spiral Hill, Emmen, Netherlands, 1971; Amarillo Ramp, Tecovas Lake, Amarillo, Texas, 1973. **Selected bibliography** M. Merleau-Ponty, *The Visible and The Invisible*, Evanston, 1968; *The Writings of Robert Smithson*, edited by N. Holt, New York, 1979; G. A. Tiberghien, *Land Art*, Paris, 1993; G. Shapiro, *Earthwards – Robert Smithson and Art after Babel*, London, 1995; *Robert Smithson: The Collected Writings*, edited by J. Flam, Berkeley, 1996; *Land and Environmental Art*, edited by J. Kastner and B. Willis, Hong Kong, 1998; *The Writings of Robert Smithson*, edited by E. Schmidt and K. Voeckler, Cologne, 2000; *After Modern Art 1945–2000*, edited by D. Hopkins, Glasgow, 2000.

Paolo Soleri

Italy
1919

Architect, town planner and sculptor. Paolo Soleri settled in the United States in 1947, and trained in Wright's studio in Taliesin. In 1955 he moved to Scottsdale, in Arizona, where he built some "earth-houses", sculpture-buildings made of poor materials. In 1961 he opened the Cosanti foundation-school turning this experimental centre into a laboratory yard open to the students of the University of Arizona, and in 1970 he founded the city of Arcosanti at Cordes Junction. Its main core is a megastructure of twenty-five storeys planned to house five thousand people, and that is still under way. Paolo Soleri was one of the first architects to become aware of the problems of ecology and that of the promotion of an architecture rooted in the natural landscape. On many occasions Soleri exhibited his models of urban structures expressly studied as forms of settlement suited to the different environmental conditions of the terrain: including the small polar village (Arcollective), the mountain hamlet (Theodiga), the water-city (Novanoah), the space town (Asteromo) and the huge production centre (Babelnoah).

Cosanti, Phoenix,
Arizona, 1961.

Works Cosanti, Phoenix, Arizona, 1961–; Arcosanti, Cordes Junction, Arizona, 1970–. **Selected bibliography** P. Soleri, *Archetipi Cosanti – Paolo Soleri architetto*, 1956; P. Soleri, *Arcology: The City in the Image of Man*, Phoenix, 1969 (1999); D. Wall, *Visionary Cities: the Arcology of Paolo Soleri*, New York, 1970; P. Soleri, *The Bridge between Matter and Spirit Is Matter Becoming Spirit*, New York, 1973; P. Soleri, *Fragments – A Selection from the Sketchbooks of Paolo Soleri: The Tiger Paradigm-Paradox*, San Francisco, 1981; P. Soleri, *The Omega Seed. An Eschatological Hypothesis*, New York, 1981, P. Soleri, *Paolo Soleri's Earth Casting: For Sculpture, Models and Construction*, Salk Lake City, 1984; P. Soleri, *Technology and Cosmogenesis*, New York, 1986; F. Ranocchi, *Paolo Soleri*, Rome, 1996; R. Pizarro, *Paolo Soleri: An Introduction to Arcology*, Phoenix, 1997.

SHODO SUZUKI

Shodo Suzuki

Japan
1934

Atami Mitsu Training Center, Atami, 1995.

Koga Folk Museum, Koga City, 1990.

Landscaper. Regarded as one of the most famous contemporary Japanese landscape designers, his creations are strongly bound to the philosophical and technical tradition of his country. In the zen tradition, the garden is above all a spiritual, mental space designed with a sophisticated care for detail that aims at evoking and glorifying nature. Shodo Suzuki's gardens are interesting for their capacity to reinterpret the principles of Japanese garden art, weaving a constant dialogue with the themes of contemporary design, both in the choice of materials (stones, raked gravel, water), and in the simultaneous contrast between feelings of anxiety, peace and hope. At Chaumont-sur-Loire for the Gardens Festival, in 1993, he created an archipelago ("Archipel") of black stones inside a *satori*—the spiritual state of the Buddhist bonze—placed upon a sea of raked white gravel like in zen temples: a symbol of the crisis in Japan and the hope for a better world.

Kawasaki International Center for Cultural Exchange, Kawasaki, 1994.

Nippon Kangyo Kakumaru Security, Chiba, 1986.

Works (a selection) Hasuda Garden, Kyoto, Japan; Hotel Katsuragawa, Kanagawa, Japan, 1983; Nippon Kangyo Kakumaru Security, Chiba, Japan, 1986; Tenri Church, Yugawa, Japan, 1989; Koga Folk Museum Garden, Koga, Japan, 1990; Toyosu ON Building Business Park, Japan, 1992; Archipel, Chaumont-sur-Loire, France, 1993; Kawasaki International Center for Cultural Exchange, Kawasaki, Japan, 1994; Atami Mitsu Training Center, Atami, Japan, 1995; Chiyoda Ward Iki Iki Plaza Ichiban-cho, Tokyo, 1995. **Selected bibliography** G. Cooper, G. Taylor, *Paradise Transformed. The Private Garden for the Twenty-First Century*, New York, 1996; *Land Forum, Process Architecture*.

TU

FRANCISCO TOLEDO

Francisco Toledo

Mexico

1940

Francisco Toledo is probably the most famous contemporary Mexican artist today. He is primarily a painter, a printmaker and a sculptor who, after working in Europe for years, decided to associate his artistic activity with the cultural rebirth of Oaxaca, a city in southern Mexico arisen in the vicinity of the Zapotec ruins of Monte Albán. Along with founding museums and art centres, and recovering the historical and architectural patrimony, Toledo also furthered the creation of a pre-Columbian ethno-botanical garden amidst the ruins of a sixteenth-century monastery. His work, influenced by Mexican history and indigenous religion, tirelessly explores the relationship between the human body and the animal world, embodying a fantastic presence and a fascination for metamorphosis, spontaneously shaping hybrid creatures, part-human, part-animal.

78

Botanical Garden,
Oaxaca, Mexico.

Exhibitions (1990–2000) "Francisco Toledo, Paintings and Watercolors 1960–89", Nohra Haime Gallery, New York, 1990; "Toledo", Latin American Masters, Los Angeles, 1991; "El mono de la tinta. Francisco Toledo", Galería del Estado, Xalapa, Veracruz, 1992; "Los cuadernos insomnes de Francisco Toledo", Aguascalientes, 1993; "Francisco Toledo, Selected Prints from the 70s", Los Angeles, 1993; "Francisco Toledo, Obra Gráfica", Guanajuato, 1994; "Francisco Toledo, Retrospective of Graphic Works", New York, 1995; "Francisco Toledo, Nuevo Catecismo para Indios Remisos et Œuvres Choisies", Paris, 1995; "Lo quel el viento a Juárez", Oaxaca, 1996; "La fragilidad del alma", Biennale di Venezia, Venice, 1997; "Insectario", Oaxaca, Culiacán, Tijuana, Celaya, Santiago de Chile, New York, 1998–2000; "Obra Gráfica 1999", Oaxaca, 1999; "Francisco Toledo. Grafica 1998–99", Mexico, Oaxaca, 1999; "Francisco Toledo", London, 2000. **Selected bibliography** T. del Conde, *Francisco Toledo*, Mexico, 1980; L. Cardoza y Aragón, *Toledo. Pintura y cerámica*, Mexico, 1987; J. L. Borges, *Manual de zoología fantástica*, Mexico, 1990; *Hechizo de Oaxaca*, Monterrey, 1991; *Historia del Arte de Oaxaca*, Oaxaca, 1997.

"You care about gardens when
you feel trust, hope in the future;
and also when you are aware
that the powers of destruction
are greater than the powers
that keep gardens alive. In the past,
not just Oaxaca but the whole world
was a garden until we began
to spread like a plague, then the
garden became smaller. The first
time Christ appeared after his
resurrection, he did so like
a custodian, in a way like a sacred
profession. Nietzsche says that one
day or another we shall realize
that what we need in our cities
is silent places, spacious, ample,
made for meditation, where we
can express ourselves in the plants
and the rocks, being able to take
ourselves on a walk in these
gardens"

BERNARD TSCHUMI

Bernard Tschumi

Switzerland

1944

Trained in Paris and Zurich, where in 1969 he graduated from the ETH, in 1983 he won the competition for the Parc de La Villette in Paris. In contrast with the spatial organization typical of the Renaissance and the nineteenth century, this park is shaped like an "open plan", a variation of the canonical modern spatial scheme. The new park is laid out in a set of three systems, each with its own logic, its own properties, and its own limits; the punctual system (*folies*, programmes), the linear system (movements) and the superficial system (open spaces). The overlaying of the various systems creates a series of tensions, carefully organized, that heighten the dynamism of the park. "Tschumi's work is opposed to the overestimated value of form, striving to reinscribe within architecture the movement of bodies in space along with the social and political realities connected with it." He has taught at various institutes, including the Architectural Association, the Institute for Architecture and Urban Studies of New York, Princeton University and Cooper Union; presently he is president of the Graduate School of Architecture, Planning and Preservation at Columbia University.

Parc de La Villette,
Paris, 1988.

Works (a selection) Parc de La Villette, Paris, 1988; Le Fresnoy National Studio for Contemporary Arts, Tourcoing, France, 1998; Lerner Hall Student Center, Columbia University, 1999; Marne-La-Vallée, Architecture School, Champs-sur-Marne, Paris, 1999; Concert Hall and Exhibition Complex, Rouen, France, 2001; Florida International University School of Architecture, Miami, Florida. **Selected bibliography** B. Tschumi, *The Manhattan Transcript: Theoretical Projects*, New York-London, 1981 (1994); B. Tschumi, *Cinégramme Folie: Le Parc de La Villette*, Princeton-Paris, 1987; B. Tschumi, *Architecture and Disjunction: Collected Essays 1975–1990*, Cambridge-London, 1994 (1998); B. Tschumi, *Event Cities (Praxis)*, Cambridge-London, 1994 (1999); B. Tschumi, *Le Fresnoy: Architecture In-Between*, New York, 1999; B. Tschumi, *Event Cities 2*, Cambridge-London, 2000.

Parc de La Villette,
Paris, 1988.

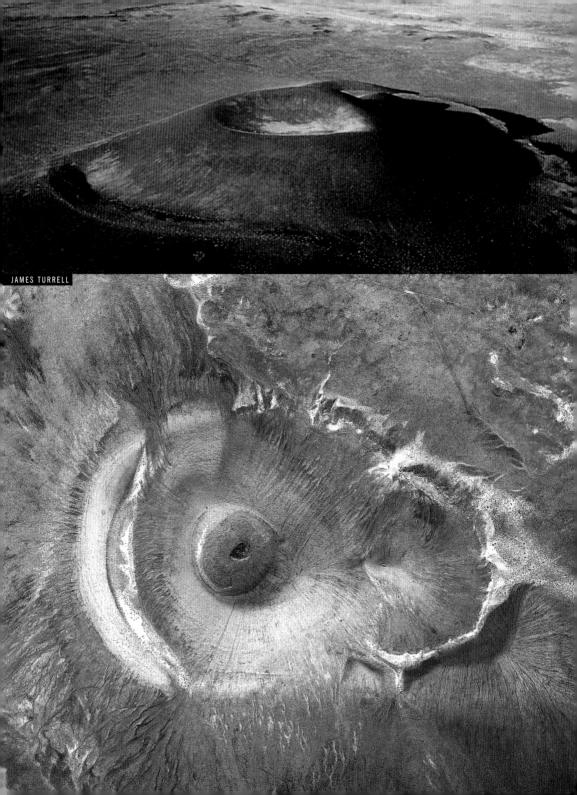

JAMES TURRELL

James Turrell

Usa

1943

After studying psychology and mathematics, in 1974 he created his first "Skyspace" and in the Arizona desert discovered the Roden Crater, a volcanic crater. In his first installations he used crisscrossed light rays, produced by halogen lamps, creating illuminated geometric forms that interact with the bareness of the surrounding space and the world outside. Using light as a material, Turrell creates perceptive experiences rather than actual representations; he exploits the physical characteristics of the environment in which he works, either in terms of their symbolic and emotional qualities, or with regards to the natural profile and the materials of the site. In 1973 he was invited to do a work in a wing of Villa Panza di Biumo at Varese and the following years, again for Giuseppe Panza di Biumo, he created a number of designs for buildings and public areas.

Roden Crater,
Flagstaff, Arizona, 1980.

Raemar, Whitney
Museum of American Art,
New York, 1980.

Skyspace 1, Villa Panza,
Varese, 1975.

Milk Run, Stroom,
The Hague, 1996.

*Projection with Halogen
Lamp*, Whitney
Musuem of Amerian Art,
New York, 1980.

One-man shows Stedelijk Museum, Amsterdam, 1976; Whitney Museum, New York, 1994; Magasin 3, Stockholm, 1994; Barbara Gladstone Gallery, New York, 1994; Contemporary Art Gallery, Art Tower Mito, Japan, 1995; Stroom, The Hague, 1996; Museum of Modern Art, Saitama, 1997; Kunsthaus, Bregenz, 1997; Nagoia City Museum, 1998; Contemporary Art Museum, Houston, 1998; Setagaia Museum, Tokyo, 1998. **Catalogues** J. Turrell, *James Turrell, Light & Space: An Exhibition*, New York, 1980; J. Turrell, *James Turrell: Four Light Installations*, Seattle, 1982; *Occluded Front, James Turrell*, edited by J. Brown, Los Angeles, 1985; C. Adcock, *James Turrell: The Roden Crater Project*, Tucson, 1986; G. Adcock, *James Turrell, The Art of Light and Space*, Berkeley-Los Angeles-Oxford, 1990; *Un choix d'art minimal dans la collection Panza: Carl André, Dan Flavin, Sol LeWitt, Robert Morris, Bruce Nauman, Richard Nonas, James Turrell, Lawrence Weiner*, Paris, 1990; J. Turrell, *James Turrell: First Light*, Stuttgart, 1991; *James Turrell: Perceptual Cells*, edited by J. Svestka, Stuttgart, 1992; R. Andrews, *James Turrell: Sensing Space*, Seattle, 1992; J. Turrell, *Air Mass / James Turrell*, London, 1993; *James Turrell*, edited by D. Menaker Rothschild, Williamstown, Mass., 1995; J. Meuris, *James Turrell: la perception est le médium*, Brussels, 1995; *James Turrell: dipinto con la luce*, edited by G. Sambonet, Milan, 1998; *James Turrell: Spirit and Light*, Houston, 1998; J. Turrell, *James Turrell, the Other Horizon*, New York, 1999.

"Looking into"

VWZ

FRANCESCO VENEZIA

Francesco Venezia

Italy
1944

The designs for the plaza of Lauro (1972), the Lauro House (1975) and the Town Hall of Taurano (1979), along with the creation of the museum of Gibellina (1981), are a few of the most significant works that focused the attention of international critics on Francesco Venezia and that illustrate his distinguished approach to design. An essential, minimal architectural idiom that we again find in his works for public areas, like the town garden of Gibellina (1984–87), the designs for Salaparuta (1986) and the outdoor theatre amidst the ruins of ancient Salemi (1989). In recent years Venezia has dealt with problems on an urban scale, including the design for the Stadthalle by the bridge on the Danube at Regensburg (1987), the renovation and arrangement of Buida Oli at Alcoy in Spain (1988–89), and the design to rehabilitate the historic centre at Salerno (1998). Since 1986 he has taught at the IUAV of Venice.

Museum of Gibellina,
Gibellina, 1981–87.

Plaza at Lauro,
Lauro, 1972.

Garden,
Gibellina, 1984–87.

Works Plaza at Lauro, Italy, 1972; Lauro House, Lauro, 1975–76; Town Hall of Taurano, Avellino, Italy, 1979–93; Museum of Gibellina, Gibellina, Italy, 1981–87; Outdoor Theatre at Salemi, Trapani, Italy, 1983–86. **Selected bibliography** F. Venezia, *La torre d'Ombre o l'architettura delle apparenze reali*, Naples, 1978; F. Venezia, *Scritti brevi*, Naples, 1990; *Francesco Venezia. Architetture in Sicilia*, edited by B. Messina, Naples, 1993; *Francesco Venezia. Due case. Tre edifici pubblici*, edited by A. Gonzales Raventos and C. Vasquez Zaldivar, Santiago del Chile, 1994; *Francesco Venezia: l'architettura, gli scritti, la critica*, edited by F. Dal Co, Milan, 1998.

Peter Walker

Usa

1932

In 1957 with Hideo Sasaki he founded Sasaki Walker Associates, and a few years later Walker and Partners. His thirty years of activity have coincided with the evolution of the arts, of urban planning and the conception of public space. Art is a part of Walker's work and a constant source of inspiration and models that, transposed in the art of landscaping, become textures, objects, compositions of complex systems. Minimalism, Land Art, abstractionism and organicism are fused in a specific art in which the colours, materials, forms unfold, revealing and transfiguring the nature and shape of places. Walker's representations are some of the most forceful and suggestive, either when they involve outside conditions, as in the desert landscape of Solana, or when they deal with the urban situation, as in the Tanner Fountain.

Toyota Municipal Museum of Art, Aichi, 1992–95.

Marina Linear Park, San Diego, California, 1989.

Principal Mutual Life Insurance Company Corporate Expansion, Des Moines, Iowa, 1996.

Works Foothill College, Los Altos, California, 1957–60; Concord Performing Arts, Concord, California, 1975; Marlboro Street Roof Garden, Boston, Massachusetts, 1979; Cambridge Center Roof Garden, Cambridge, Massachusetts, 1979; Necco Garden, Cambridge, Massachusetts, 1980; Burnett Park, Fort Worth, Texas, 1983; Institute for Advanced Biomedical Research, Portland, Oregon, 1984; Tanner Fountain, Harvard University, Cambridge, Massachusetts, 1984; Ibm Solana, Westlake and Southlake, Solana, Texas, 1984–91; Herman Miller Inc., Rockland, California, 1985; Ibm Clearlake, Houston, Texas, 1987; Harlequin Plaza, Greenwood Village, Colorado, 1988; Marina Linear Park, San Diego, California, 1989; Plaza Tower and Town Center Park, Costa Mesa, California, 1991; Ibm Japan Makuhari Building, Makuhari, Japan, 1991; Harima Science Garden City, Harima, Japan, 1991–93; Marugame Station Plaza, Marugame, Japan, 1992; Center for the Advanced Science and Technology, Harima, Japan, 1992; Toyota Municipal Museum of Art, Aichi Prefecture, Japan, 1992–95; Power Plants, Chaumont-sur-Loire, France, 1993; Kempinski Hotel, München Airport Center, Munich, Germany, 1994; Longacres Park, Renton, Washington, 1994; San Diego Library Walk, San Diego, California, 1995; Oyama Training Center, Oyama, Japan, 1995; Ayala Triangle, Manila, Philippines, 1996; Principal Mutual Life Insurance Company Corporate Expansion, Des Moines, Iowa, 1996; McConnell Foundation, Redding, California, 1997; Stralauer Platz Park, Berlin, 1998; Industrial & Commercial Bank of China, Beijing, 1998; Saitana Sky Forest Plaza, Saitama, Japan; Sony Center, Berlin; New England Aquarium, Boston, Massachusetts. **Selected bibliography** L. Jewell, *Peter Walker: Experiments in Gesture, Seriality and Flatness*, New York, 1990; *The American Landscape, Christian Zapatka*, edited by M. Zardini, New York, 1996; U. Weilacher, *Between Landscape Architecture and Land Art*, Basel, 1996; G. Cooper, G. Taylor, *Paradise Transformed. The Private Garden for the Twenty-First Century*, New York, 1996. L. Levy, *Peter Walker: Minimalist Gardens*, Washington, 1997; I. Cortesi, *Il parco pubblico. Paesaggi 1985–2000*, Milan, 2000.

*Harima Science
Garden City,*
Harima, 1991–93
(P. Palmer Photo).

*Nishi Harima
Town Park,*
Harima, 1994
(K. Kawai Photo).

*Harima Science
Garden City,*
Harima, 1991–93
(H. Mitani Photo).

Ibm Solana Headquarters,
Westlake and Southlake,
Solana, Texas, 1984–91.

RON WIGGINTON - LAND STUDIO

Ron Wigginton
Land Studio

Usa

Metaphysical Garden,
City Forest, Escondido,
California, 1985.

Ron Wigginton's designs might be interpreted as the endeavour to represent a new approach to nature, as the last act of a cultural quest beginning with the landscape painters of the nineteenth century. Wigginton, with his installations, helps us observe nature, without directly entering it. Footbridges, platforms, landing wharfs created like archetypes of a raised walkway or else, sometimes, entirely set apart from nature. So these are not designs that leave their "mark" by penetrating, carving or distorting the land, but instead are complements that merely graze the surface in order to behold that landscape, chosen as an exemplary model provided by nature. Unlike other landscapers, who seek to implicate topography more directly, the use of platforms determines a physical boundary from which to overlook nature, a completely artificial place for lingering and resting.

83

Works Six Metaphysical Gardens, The Escondido Surgery Center, Escondido, California; Starwalk, Pacific Beach, California, 1984; Studio City Forest, San Diego, California, 1985; Miraflores, Fairbanks Ranch, California, 1987; Wheat Walk, Davis, University of California, 1988; El Cajon Boulevard Revitalization Plan, San Diego; Art Gallery Metaphysical Park, City Forest, San Diego. **Selected bibliography** *The American Landscape, Christian Zapatka*, edited by M. Zardini, New York, 1996; G. Cooper, G. Taylor, *Paradise Transformed. The Private Garden for the Twenty-First Century*, New York, 1996; *Designed Landscape Forum 1*, edited by G. Crandell and E. Reifeiss, Washington, 1998.

James Wines
Site

Usa
1932

James Wine is the founder and president of Site, created in 1970. Site's long career is substantiated by over 150 designs and executions in architecture, landscape, interior design and the furnishing of exhibition spaces. They always express an environmental vision as well as a protest against the ecological disaster caused by the excessive exploitation of natural resources. In his designs this criticism calls upon abandoned icons of modernism, retrieved as a "negative" manifesto of the industrial era and incorporated so as to form a contrast with the new spaces: for instance, in the US pavilion for the Hanover Expo—conceived as a microcosm of the American landscape and where plazas and roofs are connected by a circuit recalling Route 66 that goes from Chicago to California—or in the works presented at the International Architecture Exhibition of the Venice Biennale, where our total dependance on fossil fuel is represented symbolically by a net hung on a tanker and filled with oil-stained dummies.

Highway 86, Expo '86,
Vancouver, Canada, 1986.

Avenue 5, Expo '92,
Seville, 1992.

*Tennessee Aqua
Center*, Chattanooga,
Tennessee, 1993.

La Ville Radieuse,
Biennial of Architecture,
Venice, 2000.

Works (a selection) Highway 86, Expo '86, Vancouver, Canada, 1986; Shinwa Resort, Kisokomo-Kagen, Japan, 1991; Avenue 5, Expo '92, Seville, Spain, 1992; Tennessee Aqua Center, Chattanooga, Tennessee, 1993; La Ville Radieuse, Biennial of Architecture, Venice, 2000; Usa Pavilion, Expo 2000, Hanover, Germany, 2000; Fondazione Rossini, Briosco, Italy, 2000. **Selected bibliography** De-Architecture, edited by J. Wines, New York, 1987; Site, edited by J. Wines, New York, 1989; Architecture of Ecology: Architectural Design Profile, edited by J. Wines, London, 1997; The Aesthetics of Green Architecture, edited by J. Wines,London, 1997.

Jacques Wirtz

Belgium
1924

On the scene of landscape architecture today, the works of Jacques Wirtz are impressive, less by their originality or their use of forms, materials and colours borrowed from other fields of art, than for their "faithfulness" to the tradition of the art of gardens. The use of images and forms belonging to our collective memory, the use of a traditional language, the skilful reference to topiary art and gardening, all shy away from intellectualistic distortion and technological interference: the hedges designed in geometric shapes play the customary role of composition and formal enhancement; the use of water is limited to playing with different levels and geometric shapes; the boxwood hedges are arranged in a rigid geometric system closed by rows of trees. Jacques Wirtz' designs are enriched by traditional presences such as rose beds, vegetable gardens and outdoor playgrounds. The outcome is an authentic architectural composition, extremely balanced and organized, consistent with the most tried-and-true lessons of the tradition of historic gardens.

Tuileries Gardens, Paris, 1998.

Kontich Park, Antwerp, 1988.

Garden, Hasselt, 1976.

Works (a selection) Garden, Hasselt, Belgium, 1976; Kontich Park, Antwerp, 1988; Parc, Festival du jardin, Chaumont-sur-Loire, France, 1991–92; Restoration of the Tuileries Gardens, Paris, 1998.
Selected bibliography J. Wirtz, F. Botermelk, *Le jardin privé d'un maître-sculpteur du paysage*, Paris, 1991; G. Cooper, G. Taylor, *Paradise Transformed. The Private Garden for the Twenty-First Century*, New York, 1996; G. Cooper, G. Taylor, *Garden for the Future*, New York, 2000.

"The garden is like a theatre stage"